Celebrating the Special School

Michael Farrell

David Fulton Publishers

This edition reprinted 2007 by Routledge
2 Park Square, Milton Park, Abingdon, Oxon, OX14 4RN
Simultaneously published in the USA and Canada
By Routledge
270 Madison Avenue, New York, NY 10016

First published in Great Britain in 2006 by David Fulton Publishers

10 9 8 7 6 5 4 3 2

371.9 FAR

3023934

British Library Cataloguing in Publication Data
A catalogue record for this book is available from the British Library.

ISBN: 1 84312 407 6

LEEDS TRINITY UNIVERSITY

Typeset by RefineCatch Limited, Bungay, Suffolk
Printed and bound in Great Britain

Contents

Acknowledgements

I would like to thank the organisations, local authorities, schools, parents and pupils who contributed to this book. Where descriptions of local authorities and schools are given, these were agreed with those concerned. This does not imply that the local authority or school necessarily endorses arguments put forward elsewhere in the book. Similarly, where parents and pupils expressed their views, this does not imply that they agree with views expressed elsewhere in the book.

Thanks are also due for the photographs:

Ruth Hunt (www.flickr.com/photos/kitti) took the picture of the author and bulldog 'Harry'.

Fairfields School, Northamptonshire (http://atschool.eduweb.co.uk/fair-fields/FairfieldsSchoolie.htm), gave permission to use the photographs in Chapters 1, 3 and 9.

Walton Hall School, Staffordshire, gave permission to use the pictures in Chapters 2, 4 and 7.

Barrs Court School, Hereford (www.barrscourt.hereford.sch.uk), gave permission to use the photographs in Chapters 5 and 10.

Chelfham Mill School, Devon (www.chelfhammillschool.co.uk), gave permission to use the pictures in Chapters 6 and 8.

Preface

This book celebrates the work of special schools. In doing so, I refer to LEAs that support these schools well. Parents, pupils and ex-pupils of special schools also have their say. Because the book is about celebrating the work of special schools, there are many examples of what these schools do.

So why is there a need for this book? Numerous texts already extol what they take to be the virtues of educating pupils with special educational needs (SEN) in the mainstream. Journals that purport to be about special education have played a one-track recording on inclusion in the mainstream for many years now. Yet far too little is said about the crucial work that special schools perform.

Perhaps such a book as this one would be redundant if government had a clear vision about the future of special schools. But on the contrary, government appear confused to put it at its most generous. At one point ministers seem to be floating the idea that there are moral, educational and social reasons why children should be educated in mainstream schools (Department for Education and Employment, 1997). Also, statutory guidance is produced that is far from even-handed about how to treat parents according to whether they want their child to attend a special or a mainstream school (DfES, 2001b, p.1). At another point government seems to want to say that it supports special schools.

Amid this one-sided 'debate' and confusion, good special schools up and down the country steadfastly continue their work, unnoticed, unsung and sometimes derided by those who have no conception of what a modern special school is like.

This book is an attempt to bring to the fore some of the work of the modern special school. I do not expect it to cause a moment's doubt in the mind of a single anti-special school inclusion lobbyist. But if it lifts the spirits of one young person who attends or has attended a good special school, or his parents, it will have been worthwhile. If it encourages the many dedicated professionals who work in or support special schools, this will be a bonus. Should it lead a few 'inclusion officers' in LEAs to question whether they might be losing their specialist knowledge of children with special educational needs, it would be wonderful.

Michael Farrell
Epsom
March 2006

About the Author

Dr Michael Farrell trained as a teacher and as a psychologist at the Institute of Psychiatry and has worked as a headteacher, as a lecturer at the Institute of Education, London, and as a local education authority inspector. He managed national projects for City University and for the Government Department of Education. Michael Farrell presently works as a special education consultant. This has involved policy development and training with LEAs, work with voluntary organisations, support to schools in the independent and maintained sectors, and advice to Ministries abroad. Among his books, which are translated into European and Asian languages, are:

Standards and Special Educational Needs (Continuum, 2001)

The Special Education Handbook (David Fulton, 1997, 1998, 2000, 2002)

Understanding Special Educational Needs: A Guide for Student Teachers (Routledge, 2003)

Special Educational Needs: A Resource for Practitioners (Sage, 2004)

Inclusion at the Crossroads: Concepts and Values in Special Education (Fulton, 2004)

Key Issues in Special Education: Raising Standards of Pupils' Attainment and Achievement (Routledge, 2005)

The Effective Teacher's Guide to Behavioural, Emotional and Social Difficulties (Routledge, 2006a)

The Effective Teacher's Guide to Moderate, Severe and Profound Learning Difficulties (Routledge, 2006b)

The Effective Teacher's Guide to Dyslexia and Other Specific Learning Difficulties (Routledge, 2006c)

The Effective Teacher's Guide to Autism and Other Communication Difficulties (Routledge, 2006d)

The Effective Teacher's Guide to Sensory Impairment and Physical Disability (Routledge, 2006e)

Foreword
by
Baroness Mary Warnock

It is high time that someone publicly celebrated special schools, and no one is better qualified than Michael Farrell to do so. For years government ministers and civil servants have paid grudging lip-service to special schools: 'We recognise that there will always be a place for some special schools, for children with the most profound and complex disabilities . . .'. This has put the special schools firmly at the bottom of the pile, not something that any sane parent would choose for her child; and it has perpetuated the unexamined presumption that all parents and all children prefer mainstream education. Inclusion as an intrinsic good has been at the top of the agenda. Michael Farrell's book should go a long way to redressing the balance. He gives us detailed evidence of good practice in special schools. He explains actual methods of teaching children with a wide variety of difficulties and disabilities, both demystifying the pedagogy, and showing what a high degree of expertise and specialist skill is required for such teaching. He describes schools that cater for children with profound disabilities, such as the deaf/blind, but also for children with moderate learning difficulties, and disabilities that are primarily emotional and behavioural; and he makes it clear how many children have more than one kind of need. This sort of evidence is extremely difficult to come by, and is therefore of immense value. So is the evidence derived from the testimony of parents and of pupils and former pupils of the schools.

I profoundly believe that for many children, not only those with the most severe or multiple disabilities, special schools are their salvation. They can trust their teachers to understand their difficulties and they can be free from the teasing and bullying that they fear from their fellow pupils (and this fear is more intense for those children who are not visibly or obviously disabled, such as those with autism in its various degrees). One of the huge advantages of a special school for such children is that it is small. In a small school, a child knows everyone and is known by all the staff. The staff, too, know one another and work in a collegiate atmosphere, where they can share their insights and their problems. Special schools are, of course, not cheap. But the policy of inclusion in mainstream schools should not be cheap either if it is to provide enough support for individual pupils to enable them to flourish. It is not enough that children with special needs in mainstream schools should be supported by teaching assistants; they need expert, trained teachers, who can teach them in small groups, or one-to-one. This is something that few mainstream schools can offer. What has been wrong with the policy of inclusion has been the idea that if some children with special needs can flourish in the mainstream they all can.

Michael Farrell's book should be compulsory reading for ministers and civil servants who are responsible for schools policy. There are some signs that the orthodoxy of inclusion may be showing cracks. There are, for example, thirty schools up and down the country officially known as Maintained Specialist Non-Mainstream Schools, mostly for pupils with moderate learning difficulties, all of whom have Statements of Educational Need. These schools specialise in IT or sport or drama. They are special schools under a new and cumbersome name. They are immensely sought after by parents, and they are small. I wish them well. Perhaps after reading this book ministers may be brave enough to rechristen them Special Schools.

Mary Warnock

March 2006

Special Schools and Inclusion

What is inclusion?

The term 'inclusion' is often used to refer to efforts to educate an increasing number of pupils with special educational needs (SEN) in mainstream schools and fewer in special schools. Some maintain steadfastly that special schools are oppressive, infringe equal opportunities, deny human rights, and are immoral. Others argue passionately for the support and development of special schools where they believe children have the opportunity of a better academic and personal education than in mainstream.

For every disability lobbyist crying 'segregation' there are parents marching to the town hall with banners raised for the continuation of their local special school. To say inclusion is an emotive topic is rather like saying that Genghis Khan had the occasional bad day.

Yet at the heart of calls for the ultimate closure of special schools, lies a diminution of the importance of providing the best education possible for children, including children with SEN. The danger is that inclusion will come to be seen as more central to the work of schools than education.

The potential negative consequences of this can be recognised if one pictures a fire service that has become too focused on being inclusive. It is neither homophobic nor racist and treats male and female employees with equal respect. Social class is no barrier to recruitment or promotion and officers may be of any religious minority. Unfortunately, when the fire officers arrive at a major conflagration, they discover that they have misunderstood where the nearest water supply is. Once this is resolved they find that the hose is too short to reach the blaze properly and anyway it leaks so that the water pressure is insufficient to control the inferno. In other words, they are just not very good at putting fires out. This is because in striving to be inclusive, which is a secondary feature of their work, they have overlooked their main purpose, indeed the reason why they were constituted, which is to extinguish fires.

It is not hard to imagine similar situations in other services. A welcoming hospital in which patients tend not to get better and where it is possible for a baby to be admitted for a minor ailment and die from an infection contracted there. Or a transport service where the speed at which equality of opportunity for staff is pursued exceeds that of the trains and buses that they operate and where arriving at one's destination on time is a bonus. It is also not difficult to envisage an education service in which a child making good progress in academic achievement and in personal and social development comes a poor second to inclusion in a mainstream school.

Unfortunately, at a time when it is essential to have a clear vision for SEN, inclusion and special schools, the policy of the Labour government is confused. This is in part because concern to improve the education of pupils with SEN and the so-called inclusion/diversity 'agenda' are often incompatible. The core feature of schools is to provide high-quality education as indicated by pupils learning something worthwhile and evidence that they have done so. The prime feature of schools cannot be inclusion; it must be education. Where good education in a special school is considered not as a prime aim but as something that should be bargained against an inclusion agenda, trouble looms for pupils with SEN and their parents. Special schools come to be seen as a revolving door to get pupils with SEN back to mainstream where they supposedly really belong. Or special schools are seen as holding places offering pupils a second-best 'segregated' provision while ordinary schools sort themselves out sufficiently to be able to provide for them.

Mary Warnock (2005) has pointed to the blame that can be attached to certain politicians, ministers and civil servants in lowering the esteem in which special schools are held in some quarters. She has also indicated examples of the high quality of special schools. Special schools should not be seen as places of last resort. Also, she argues, mainstream schools are not the ideal provision for all learners but can be settings in which children can be isolated, marginalised, unhappy and disaffected.

The legal position on inclusion and statutory guidance

The confusion around special schools and inclusion is further illustrated by the tensions within the legal position on inclusion, how it is sometimes mis-understood and how statutory guidance further muddies the water. The Special Educational Needs and Disability Act 2001 amended the Education Act 1996 section 316 (3) with regard to children who have a 'statement' of SEN. The amendment indicates that a child with a statement must be educated in a mainstream school unless this is incompatible with parents' wishes or with other children receiving an efficient education. The amendment is set out below.

> If a statement is maintained under section 324 for the child, he must be educated in a mainstream school unless that is incompatible with:
>
> (a) the wishes of his parent, or
>
> (b) the provision of efficient education for other children.

This does not mean however that, if the education of a child with SEN is incompatible with the efficient education of other pupils, mainstream education can be flatly turned down. It can only be refused if there are no reasonable steps that can be taken to prevent the incompatibility. Of course, it may not be possible to take steps to prevent a child's inclusion being incompatible with the efficient education of others. For example a child's behaviour may systematically, persistently and significantly threaten the safety or impede the learning of others. Or the teacher, even with other support, may have to spend a greatly disproportionate amount of time with the child with SEN in relation to the rest of the class.

These are not the only caveats however. There are others that arise when one comes to consider a particular mainstream school, rather than the generic concept of 'the mainstream'. If a parent expresses a preference for a particular mainstream school to be named in their child's statement of SEN, schedule 27 of the Education Act 1996 comes into effect. This requires the LEA to name the parents' preferred choice of school in the child's statement unless any of three conditions apply. These are:

1 The school cannot provide for the needs of the child.
2 The child's inclusion at the school would be incompatible with the efficient education of other pupils.
3 The child's inclusion at the school would be incompatible with the efficient use of resources.

Legal caveats apply then to placing a child in 'the mainstream' and to placing a child in a particular mainstream school. These are sometimes not understood by commentators. For example in an article on 'inclusive education' (Sheehy, Rix, Nind and Simmons, 2004), the authors, Open University lecturers, state that the Special Educational Needs and Disability Act 2001 amended the Education Act 1996 and, 'removed all but one of the caveats that had acted as a barrier to inclusion' (p.138). In fact, this ignores caveats that relate to a particular school rather than the generic concept of 'mainstream'.

At the same time that the SEN and Disability Act 2001 maintains caveats regarding inclusion, the statutory guidance document *Inclusive Schooling: Children with Special Educational Needs* (DfES, 2001b) betrays a lack of even-handedness towards parents wanting a special school education for their child. The publication states, 'where parents want a mainstream education for their child *everything possible should be done to provide it*'. Equally where parents want a special school place *'their wishes should be listened to and taken into account'* (DfES, 2001b, p.1, italics added). The difference between 'everything possible' being done regarding parents wanting mainstream while parents who want a special school are only 'listened to' is made more stark by the inappropriate juxtaposition of the word 'equally' between the two unequal commitments.

Chapter 2 of this book further discusses inclusion and problems with the approach in relation to special schools. The next section prepares the ground by reminding readers of the three types of special schools to be found in England.

Types of special schools in England

Special schools in England may be maintained, non-maintained or independent.

Maintained special schools can be either community or foundation schools. A community special school is a state school that is wholly owned and maintained by the LEA. A foundation special school is a type of state school that has more freedom than a community school to manage itself and decide on its admissions, the governing body being the employer and the admissions authority. Although a foundation special school's land and buildings are owned by the governing body or a charitable foundation, funding comes from the LEA, which also pays for any building work.

The support of LEAs for maintained special schools is variable. An LEA that does value its special schools is Staffordshire, whose work is described below, followed by an account of one of the maintained schools that it supports.

Staffordshire LEA

The special schools in Staffordshire LEA have staff members who are mentors and assessors for the Inclusion Quality Mark and the Basic Skills Quality Mark. Special schools are involved in Well Being Projects, Investment in People and Health Promoting Schools awards. Some special schools have achieved Arts Marks and Sports Marks. One special school, a Leading Edge School and specialist technology college, helps support other schools. Advance Skills teachers in special schools support special and mainstream staff in areas such as information and communications technology and basic skills teaching. A special school headteacher is the PIVATs consultant for the county while a special school senior teacher is the county consultant for B Squared. (PIVATs and B Squared are finely graded assessments.) A special school head of care co-ordinates the manual handling team and the related county training programme. The four special schools for pupils with physical disability in the LEA provide outreach support for the county. LEA officers and special school staff are liaising with the Specialist Schools and Academies Trust to seek specialist status for some of these schools.

Staffordshire LEA supports its special schools in various ways. In 2005, there was a review of special school provision which led to proposals to move from having eight schools for pupils with severe learning difficulties and eight schools for pupils with moderate learning difficulties to having generic special primary and secondary special schools for pupils with moderate or severe learning difficulties. In relation to this, the LEA has sought to work closely with special school headteachers, governors, and relevant units within the offices of the director of education. A Targeted Capital Fund bid has been made for a new secondary special school and for a community vocational centre. The LEA has invested in the development of 'well-being rooms', by matching money from three schools with money from the Standards Fund for training resources and advisor time. The well-being rooms are to help in the nurturing of emotionally vulnerable children, and many of these groups take place in special schools.

Various working groups reflect the involvement of special school staff in the workings of the LEA. In a 'Challenging Needs' group, members are headteachers of special schools, social care workers, residential setting managers, health workers, LEA officers and others. This group followed from the building of three enhanced units attached to special schools for pupils that formerly might have been educated outside the authority and the group help support staff, pupils and parents. A data group, which issues a termly newsletter, comprises members from special schools and others including members of the education research advisory team (part of the school improvement team). Headteachers of schools for pupils with behavioural, emotional and social difficulties (BESD) are key members of a steering group that is informing a review of provision for pupils with BESD and this group liaises with a regional advisor. A working party concerning outreach work for pupils with physical disability includes headteachers of special schools and others. There are monthly meetings of heads of care in special schools and LEA officers to support schools with work connected with Commission for Social Care Inspections and monitoring. Special school headteachers are members of all placement panels within districts of the county. Special schools are represented in all county-led (LEA) working groups for instance, local management of special school meetings, primary and secondary headteachers' meetings, the school's organisational committee, and the Joint Advisory Body. Also, special school headteachers are involved in all appointments of senior staff in the LEA.

The LEA is supporting a pilot project developing the provision of circle time for pupils with severe or profound and multiple learning difficulties working with special schools. The LEA has invested in the training of trainers for the Strategy for Crisis Intervention and Prevention (SCIP) approach so that trainers are able to help with the development and implementation of behaviour policies, preventative strategies, risk assessment and restraint. The LEA provides training leading to qualification as a Teaching and Education of Autistic Children and Communication Handicap (TEACCH) trainer and facilitator (an approach associated particularly with provision for pupils with autistic spectrum disorder). It offers training for interveners using the Picture Exchange Communication System (PECS) approach; anger management; behaviour management and a one-day accredited course in counselling skills. There is investment to support the training of special school staff to fulfil the Commission for Social Care Inspection requirements.

In seeking to ensure that special schools are kept informed, the LEA is involved in issuing a termly 'Nurture Newsletter' (relating to provision of nurture groups); a termly SEN newsletter sent to mainstream and special schools and whose editorial team includes a special school headteacher; and termly emailed updates. LEA officers work with special school staff and others in developing publications such as booklets on 'Manual Handling Guidance and Qualified Manual Handling Teams', 'B Squared Assessment', a booklet relating to provision for pupils with profound and multiple learning difficulties, and a publication on 'Challenging Needs' which encapsulates the LEA's multi-agency work.

Walton Hall School, Staffordshire

Walton Hall School, Staffordshire, a community day and weekly boarding co-educational special school for 128 pupils aged 5 to 19 years with moderate learning difficulties, is set in Victorian parkland and has specialist facilities for technology, science and music. It has playing fields, a small farm and an adventure play area. The school is organised into primary and secondary departments and there is a special nurture class for children who are emotionally vulnerable and a unit for pupils with autism.

For children at Key Stage 1, the curriculum focuses on language, pre-reading and pre-number work, using information and communications technology and support from a speech and language therapist and physiotherapist as necessary. Children aged 5 to 11 follow the National Curriculum with an emphasis on small group and individual tutorial work. Classes have up to 12 children. At secondary age (11 to 16 years), the curriculum emphasises building confidence, independence and initiative and includes work experience, an independent living programme, careers guidance, leisure activities, college placement, schools council and other features. Post-16 courses are open to pupils from local mainstream and special schools and offer a programme of activities to develop life skills and further development of literacy and numeracy, through work experience, independent living, residential camps, mini-farm and mini-enterprise, leading to Entry level qualifications, Initial and GNVQ awards.

Among the strengths of the school is its tracking of the pupils' academic progress and personal and social development using PIVATs, a finely graded assessment developed by Lancashire LEA. The school has developed a database with enabling macros for tracking the primary and secondary needs of its pupils. Results inform school development, planning, targets and the evaluation process. Pupils' year-on-year progress can be identified through the increase in PIVATs scores, reading and mathematics 'ages' and the percentage of pupil targets met.

Non-maintained special schools, as their name suggests, are not maintained by an LEA. They are non-profit-making schools operated by a charitable trust and approved as special schools under the Education Act 1996. The funding for non-maintained special schools (NMSS) comes mainly from fees charged to LEAs who place children there. NMSS are subject to regulations, which concern conditions for initial and continuing approval by the Secretary of State. These relate to such matters as governance, premises, health and safety and welfare. An example of a non-maintained school is St Margaret's School, The Children's Trust in Surrey, described below.

St Margaret's School, Surrey

St Margaret's School, The Children's Trust, Surrey (www.thechildrenstrust.org.uk) is a co-educational non-maintained residential school for pupils with profound and multiple learning difficulties aged 5 to 19 years. The school is open for 48 weeks a year and has its own doctor and team of nurses providing 24-hour medical cover. Among the innovations that the school has developed is very detailed curriculum and assessment documentation for the areas of sensory motor development.

The sensory cognitive curriculum is designed to encourage sensory awareness in sensory modes that are relevant to the individual pupil and to develop exploratory play that leads to the child involving himself in his surroundings and becoming more aware of them. An aim of the communication curriculum is to develop intentional communication enabling the child to gain some degree of autonomy, control and choice. The social curriculum promotes a child's awareness of herself and of others and develops ways of interacting with others. Included in the motor curriculum is facilitating normal movement and function, the use of physiotherapy equipment, positioning, and enabling hand movements. The life skills curriculum incorporates cognitive, communicative, motor and social skills into daily living activities so that the child has the optimum opportunity to anticipate what is about to happen and participate.

An extended curriculum provides various activities in which learning occurs, and includes religious education, creative and leisure activities, topic work, discrete modules of work and activities linked to the National Curriculum. A detailed assessment format using code letters enables aspects of learning and development to be recorded according to whether a skill is being worked towards (W), is evident (E), has been achieved (A), is generalised to other situations (G) or is measured formally as having been securely achieved.

Independent special schools are funded by pupil fees and may be run for profit. They may be approved by the Secretary of State under the Education Act 1996 as suitable for the admission of children with statements of SEN. The schools are also subject to a registration procedure for independent schools. An independent school having 25% of its pupils with statements is treated as a special school.

LEAs place most pupils and meet the costs but parents may pay the fees privately. If a special school is not approved, the Secretary of State has to consent before an LEA can place pupils with statements of SEN in the school. Regulations relating to the approval of independent schools set out conditions for initial and continued approval. They concern such matters as fitness of the school proprietors and staff, exclusions, health and welfare, the school prospectus and religious education.

Coxlease School, Hampshire

Coxlease School (www.coxleaseschool.co.uk) near Lyndhurst, Hampshire, is an independent residential school set within 10 acres of woodland in the New Forest area and offers up to 52 weeks per year provision for 50 pupils aged 9 to 17 years with severe behavioural, emotional and social difficulties. It has 200 staff and provides education, care, therapy, welfare, support and related services. On-site leisure activities include a sports hall, swimming pool, BMX and motorcycle tracks and an adventure play area. The school also has a dedicated Outdoor Education Department that offers a range of outdoor and adventurous activities for pupils and other schools.

Coxlease is organised into Junior, Middle and Senior Departments and class sizes are between three and five pupils with at least two adults in each class, all following the National Curriculum. Each pupil has an Individual Placement, Behaviour and Education plan targeting reintegration at the earliest opportunity. Six care bases are located on the school site and three more nearby in Southampton, where all pupils have single rooms. Therapeutic intervention involves therapists and counsellors either full-time or on a session basis including psychologists (both clinical and educational), art psychotherapists, social workers, counsellors and a child and adolescent psychiatrist.

Indications of the quality of special schools and the number of pupils they educate

The previous section having given examples of the types of special schools in England, this final section gives an indication of the quality of special schools and the number of pupils educated in them.

For all special schools, the school's current Office for Standards in Education (OfSTED) report gives a picture of its performance in areas such as self-evaluation and leadership and management as well as the context of pupil's attainment, achievement and progress. For maintained special schools, a further indication of the school's provision is data on the pupils' progress that have been collected and collated by the LEA (see, for example, the work of Hampshire LEA in Chapter 5).

There are also indications of the quality of non-maintained and independent special schools.

- In a pilot study in 2004, the DfES worked with 185 schools including 31 special schools, to calculate 'value added' for pupils' progress. Two special schools, Mary Hare School and RNIB New College, were first and second respectively for value added from KS2 to end of KS4 for the whole pilot (NASS, 2005a).
- Secondary School Achievement and Attainment Tables 2004, for value added from KS2 to age 15 years, indicated that 18 non-maintained NASS member schools achieved progress placing them in the top 5% of schools (NASS, March, 2005b).
- In 2004, data from current OfSTED reports indicated the quality of education in 85 of approved *independent* special schools for pupils' progress and achievement, the quality of teaching and learning and the curriculum. In 78% all standards were satisfactory or better (although this indicates too many were unsatisfactory).
- Similar data in 2005 for 63 *non-maintained* special schools indicated in practically all standards were satisfactory or better (www.nasschools.org.uk).

How many pupils are educated in special schools in England? *The National Statistics First Release* (Department for Education and Skills, 2005 – hereafter *SFR24/2005*), provides data on pupils with SEN in England.

- In the year 2005, there were 85,350 pupils on the roll of maintained special schools and 4,870 pupils in non-maintained special schools (*SFR24/2005* Table 1b).
- Additionally, 6,290 pupils with statements of SEN were educated in independent special schools (*SFR24/2005* Table 2 'Children with statements in January 2005' (f)).
- A further 1,970 pupils were dually registered with a maintained special school and an ordinary school but mainly educated in the special school (Annual Schools Census, Special Schools – number of pupils by registration type January 2005, England).

Therefore, the total of pupils educated in special schools in England is 98,480 – a figure that has remained comparatively stable in recent years (although the total for 2004 was 100,190).

While there is publicity around special schools closing, it seems counter-intuitive that there are similar numbers of pupils being educated in special schools year on year. But where in some areas special schools are closing, in others new ones are opening. Also, in some instances, what appears to be the closure of a special school is in fact the combining of two former special schools to become one split-site special school with the same number of pupils but one senior management team.

Again, it might seem incompatible with stable numbers in special schools to find that the proportion of pupils considered to have SEN in mainstream school has increased while the proportion in special schools has decreased. However, proportions are not the same as numbers of pupils. Proportions can change, for example, if more pupils considered to have SEN are found in mainstream schools, perhaps assisted by insecure procedures of identification and assessment. They can change if the severity of SEN increases so that mainstream schools have some pupils that might have formerly been taught in special schools while special schools increasingly educate children with even more severe SEN.

Even while overall numbers of pupils educated in special schools appear comparatively stable, there are worries about access to a range of special schools in some parts of England. One reason may be the confused nature of government policy and lack of even-handedness in its guidance. Another may be a feeling that government is allowing local authorities in some parts of England to pursue an agenda that is antagonistic to special schools effectively denying parents any real choice of special or mainstream school because of special school closures.

Thinking points

Readers may wish to consider:

- whether in their local area, there is a choice for parents of a range of good special schools;

- what structures and processes would need to be in place to enable a special school to demonstrate that the progress, achievement and personal and social development of its pupils was better than they would experience in a mainstream classroom or unit.

Key texts

1 Farrell, M. (2003) *The Special School Handbook*, London, David Fulton Publishers.

As an introduction to some of the issues relating to special schools. Readers may wish to refresh their memory by consulting entries on 'local education authority', 'local education authority policy framework', 'non-maintained special school', 'hospital school', 'residential therapy', 'special school', and similar topics. Appendices cover: legislation and related reports and consultation documents from the 'Warnock Report' to the present day, selected regulations from 1981 to the present, and selected circulars and circular letters from 1981 to the present and the SEN Codes of Practice 1994 and 2001.

2 Farrell, M. (2005b) *Inclusion at the Crossroads: Special Education – Concepts and Values*, London, David Fulton Publishers.

This book seeks to illustrate how aspects of special education can be better understood in the context of certain ideas and values that partly underpin them. For example, a consideration of 'self-interest and co-operation' is taken to illuminate issues relating to 'funding through school clusters'. In particular, readers may find chapter 8, 'Including Pupils with SEN: Duties and Rights', of interest.

2

From Inclusion to Optimal Education

In the previous chapter, I touched on inclusion in the sense of advocating fewer pupils with SEN in special schools and more in mainstream schools. I maintained it would be counterproductive to set inclusion above achievement and personal and social development as an educational value.

This chapter indicates further weaknesses in the arguments for inclusion in relation to: social views of SEN; moral claims for inclusion; and empirical evidence. I then outline an alternative, optimal education, shifting the core concern of schools from inclusion to education.

Social views of SEN

(a) Oppression and exclusion

Are pupils in special schools oppressed and excluded? Within a social perspective, anti-discrimination theory maintains that certain groups in society do not have equal opportunities partly because they are discriminated against and oppressed. Therefore, to challenge discrimination encourages equal opportunity.

It is assumed that groupings, social relationships and institutions are important in the distribution of power, status and opportunities. Discrimination is considered to reflect structured inequalities and reinforce them. Because society is stratified, inequalities are part of the fabric of society and underpin the social order. In this perspective, institutional oppression does not only derive from individual actions. It is often built into structural patterns, institutional patterns and organisational policies. The anti-discriminatory view is that this should be changed in the drive towards perceived equality of opportunity.

Hence the terms 'prejudice', 'discrimination' and 'oppression' arise (see panel below). For example, a fuller understanding of racism and sexism are thought to come from not only recognising personal **prejudice** but also the '**discriminatory** and **oppressive** culture base manifesting itself in and through individual thought and action' (Thompson, 2001, p.23, bold added). Tackling discrimination, therefore, involves people collectively '*challenging the dominant discriminatory culture and ideology* . . .' (p.25, italics in original). This should, it is hoped, undermine the structures that support, and are supported by, that culture.

Prejudice is seen as: 'an opinion or judgement formed without considering the relevant facts or arguments; a biased and intolerant attitude towards particular people or social groups; . . . a rigid form of thinking based on stereotypes and discrimination' (Thompson, 2001, p.35).

Discrimination refers to: 'unfair or unequal treatment of individuals or groups; prejudicial behaviour acting against the interests of those people who characteristically tend to belong to relatively powerless groups in the social structure' (p.33).

Oppression means: 'inhuman or degrading treatment of individuals or groups; hardship and injustice brought about by the dominance of one group over another; the negative and demeaning use of power. Oppression often involves disregarding the rights of an individual or group and is thus a denial of citizenship' (p.34).

Social divisions explored from this perspective have included:

- gender (Richardson and Robinson, 1997)
- ethnicity (Skellington, 1996)
- age (Thompson, 1995)
- sexual identity (Wise, 2000)
- class (Jones, 1998)
- religious creed (Brewer, 1991)
- linguistic group (Bellin, 1994)
- mental health problems (Thompson, 1998).

Further social divisions are implicit in groupings considered to need inclusion and therefore presumably assumed to be prone to exclusion such as:

- girls and boys
- minority ethnic groups
- minority faith groups
- travellers
- asylum seekers
- refugees
- pupils who need support to learn English as an additional language
- gifted and talented pupils
- children looked after by the local authority
- sick children
- young carers
- children from families under stress
- pregnant school girls
- teenage mothers
- pupils at risk of disaffection and exclusion (OfSTED, 2000, p.1).

It is perhaps not surprising to find that the 'social division' of disability (Oliver, 1996) and mental impairment (Thompson, 2001) have been identified. Also, pupils with SEN have been considered prone to exclusion (OfSTED, 2000, p.1). Finding so many supposedly oppressed and potentially excluded groups in society is part of the agenda for combating what is thought to be discrimination and contributing to more equality of opportunity. As more and more of these groupings are found, a point must be reached where the whole approach is no longer viable. Inflation strains credibility, leading people to ask how many oppressed groups can be found in a society before the bizarre situation is reached where everyone is oppressed or excluded and there is nobody left to oppress or exclude them.

Given this increasing lack of credibility, it can be argued that it is not being educated in a special school that might oppress pupils. The main oppression and exclusion that pupils in special school and their parents have to fear is that of political correctness seeking to force an over-zealous inclusion agenda even if it means denying the child a good education.

(b) Equality of opportunity and special schools

Where pupils in special schools are depicted as oppressed and not having equal opportunities, this prejudges the matter of providing the best education for these pupils. The approach to equality of opportunity for pupils with SEN is not identical to that for people of different racial groups, social-occupational classes or gender.

Consider the parent of a pupil who is a member of a minority ethnic group in a particular country who expresses a preference for a place in a mainstream school. Normally, the child should have an equal chance of getting a place as a child in a similar position who is not a member of a minority ethnic group. Ensuring equal opportunities might involve checking that the selection procedures are fair. The assumption is that ethnicity should not normally be a factor in allowing the child to take advantage of the education the school offers.

However, the case of a child with severe learning difficulties is different. A parent may express a preference for a mainstream education for their child, and that child may subsequently be educated in a mainstream school. This might be said to represent equal opportunity for the child to attend the school compared with other children who did not have severe SEN.

But would it offer an equal opportunity for the child to receive a good or even an appropriate education or for the child to be 'included' in any sense remotely connected with the usual meaning of the term? It would be a sorry state of affairs if all that was being offered in this brave new world was the equal opportunity to be marginalised.

(c) Participation in decision-making

A social perspective of SEN tends to emphasise the social origins of difficulties and disabilities and the social, financial and other disadvantages faced by people experiencing them. Such views in which people with a disability are seen as 'oppressed' (eg Abberley, 1987) have often really been about physical disability and sensory impairment highlighting the social layer of negative attitudes thought to overlay and compound these.

While the perspective may apply in some degree to physical disability and sensory impairment, it does not explain what might be the social origins of having a severe physical brain trauma leading to profound and multiple learning difficulties. Indeed it is said that social views have, 'marginalised people with intellectual disabilities' (MacKay, 2002, p.161). Of course any newly qualified teacher recognises that negative social attitudes may compound a given difficulty or disability. But to suggest that these are the primary cause of the difference, impairment or disability is unconvincing to say the least.

However, attempts have also been made (Armstrong, 2003) to relate a socially constructed view of learning difficulty to the supposed subordination and oppression of those so labelled and to an emancipatory view of 'resistance'. Armstrong collected the 'life stories' of 40 people who had been 'labelled' as having learning difficulties. Just over half of these experienced their schooling 30 years or more prior to the research. Of the remainder, ten participants attended school between 1975 and 1984 and only nine were at school after 1985.

In line with much of the anti-discrimination theory outlined earlier, Armstrong maintains that the participants experienced 'subordination' but also showed 'resistance'. These two elements he suggests offer insights into the development of special education policy. Such resistance indicates 'a struggle for emancipated spaces amidst the controlling power of the institutions of public order' (p.91). The supposed evidence of 'subordination' did not imply that participants' experiences of special schooling were unhappy, far from it. One participant in particular, 'tells a story of his schooling that is filled with fond and happy memories' (p.60).

But the impact of the label of learning difficulties, applied through special education, is believed to have led to the 'possibility' of their being controlled by others at important points in their lives. Referring to the notion of 'life world' (Habermas, 1987, passim), Armstrong suggests that, 'Through the identification of deficits and treatment by technical learning, the special school has taken over those spaces in everyday life in which people managed their own identities by social and political communication . . . Dominant ideologies are transmitted not simply within schools but through the social ordering of the education system' (p.92). Armstrong unfortunately does not explain what 'treatment by technical learning' might mean or give any examples of it.

Regarding citizenship, the label of learning difficulties is regarded as a means of managing and controlling a 'troublesome minority' (p.103). Schooling was seen as a key arena in which future participation or a lack of it 'was imposed or negotiated' (p.106). The labels created by special education were 'markers of deficiencies that legitimated the denial of citizenship' (p.123).

Armstrong's concern seems to be mainly about possible subordination. But, as Mary Warnock (2005) has pointed out, mainstream schools can be settings where children with SEN can be isolated, marginalised, unhappy and disaffected. Armstrong's points hardly read like a sustainable criticism of special schools, but more like a call for all schools, ordinary and special, to take greater account of the views of pupils/students and involve them more in decisions affecting their lives.

Also, many pupils identified as having SEN speak highly of their special school. Others who have attended special schools have gone on to participate in society, appearing to benefit from the special educational provision that accompanied the identification (see examples in Chapter 4 below).

Moral claims for inclusion

(a) The devaluation of rights

Some commentators might consider it morally desirable that a pupil with SEN be educated in a mainstream school. This moral view is unaffected by empirical evidence since the claim is that it is morally right *in itself* to adopt a policy for inclusion whatever the consequences, educational or otherwise. Such a claim might seek support in the notion of rights, arguing that children with SEN (through their parents' expression of a school preference) have a moral and/or human right to be educated in the mainstream. But is such a 'human rights' position tenable?

For John Locke (1690 – many editions) the 'rights of Man' were very few: life, liberty and property and the reserve right of overthrowing a government that did not secure these 'natural' rights. In contrast, there are presently a huge and increasing number of supposed rights. While these echo the more fundamental nature of rights found in Locke, they are now so numerous that their strength as something unalienable is rapidly eroding.

Every group that can define itself as a minority or socially position itself as oppressed appears to be able to argue for some localised form of social justice and claim rights. Perusal of almost any daily newspaper reveals further rights, such as the retired police officer reported to be mounting a legal fight over protected trees that are 'infringing his basic human right to watch satellite television' (Sapsted, 2004). At some point, concern must arise that inflation is leading to devaluation.

(b) Inclusion as a right: Wants, contradictions and rejection

Some writers such as Gallagher (2001) claim that the moral basis of inclusion is one of 'rights'. Such a claim faces the difficulty that it is yet one more piece in the avalanche of supposed rights. At their worst these are merely a politically acceptable way of someone saying they want something without the need to justify the claim or the consequences (for example by reference to empirical evidence on inclusion).

Also, because there are so many 'rights' they are becoming contradictory. For example it is claimed that deaf children have a 'right' to be included in a mainstream rather than a special school – the latter being considered by some people to be segregating and oppressive. At the same time some deaf people are claiming a 'human right' to have deaf children educated together in a special school where they can communicate with one another because they are a linguistic minority.

If supposed rights to inclusion in mainstream school are not met, this is sometimes taken to imply 'discrimination' or 'segregation'. The term 'segregation' is evocative of the enforced separate schooling of black children in the southern states of the United States of America prior to the 1960s. But it does not have quite the same ring when parents are pressing for special school places for their children. If the right to inclusion in a mainstream school is so self-evidently good, it is difficult to explain why tens of thousands of parents of children with SEN reject it.

(c) Respect and fairness

A moral claim may be made that inclusion involves treating pupils with respect and refusing to make them feel different or marginalised. However, this fails to distinguish between morally appropriate and morally inappropriate differential treatment. The challenge is to ensure that acknowledging real difference (such as that between a pupil with autism and a pupil who does not have autism) is not confused with being patronising nor regarded as marginalising. Acknowledging difference is not the same as lack of respect (Barrow, 2001, pp.239–40).

The notion of inclusion also invokes the principle of fairness, the view that, 'it is morally wrong, in itself, to treat individuals differently without providing relevant reasons for so doing'. But in such a view everything depends on what constitutes relevant reasons. These in turn depend on the particular context being considered and have to be established by independent reasoning. To put it another way, whether behaviour is 'fair' is determined by reference to other substantive moral values and the facts of a particular situation. However, fairness can still be a vital part of a coherent moral viewpoint (ibid. pp.236–7).

Unfortunately, as a principle of school practice, inclusion might well lead to or involve unfairness. For example, a class may be designated and designed for pupils with certain prior knowledge, skills and understanding. These effectively have become the relevant criteria for admission. Pupils may enter a class pursuing a two-year General Certificate of Education (GCSE) course having reached a level of understanding, skill and knowledge that makes it realistic that they will gain at least a grade in the proposed GCSE examination. To take in to such a class pupils who do not meet these criteria involves unfairness because pupils are being treated identically for no good reason, which is as partial as treating pupils differently for no good reason.

It is not fair to base one's treatment of pupils on irrelevant criteria. It is not fair to refuse to recognise differences that may be relevant in relation to the most effective and suitable way of educating a pupil. Therefore it is not in itself morally right to adopt a policy of inclusion. Inclusion itself is an unfair policy involving a refusal to discriminate on seemingly relevant criteria.

This does not mean that inclusion cannot be justified in certain circumstances, but that to do so would involve further reasons. The question of inclusion must be placed in the relevant context, which is likely to relate to some assessment of the ability of typical teachers and the purpose of educating pupils. Inclusion in a mainstream school may be better for pupils with one type of SEN and worse for pupils with other types of SEN. Given that there is no universal answer to the question of whether inclusion is worth pursuing, we should take each issue on its own and try to resolve it from an educational standpoint.

Empirical evidence

The complex nature of inclusion makes researching it difficult. An obvious preliminary to carrying out research and comparing it with earlier findings is that one is clear about what it is one is researching. Where there are so many definitions of inclusion, it is necessary for the researcher to specify the children being considered and the form that the inclusion is taking. Among important parameters are the child's age and type of SEN. For example different issues are likely to arise if one is looking at the inclusion of young children with moderate learning difficulties or much older students with severe behavioural, emotional and social difficulties. However, there have been attempts to gather empirical evidence on inclusion.

Considering pupils with 'mild disabilities', Marston (1996) compared the effects of inclusion only, the withdrawal of pupils only, and a combined service, finding higher increases in reading attainment for pupils in the combined service.

Also looking at pupils with 'mild disabilities' Manset and Semmel (1997) reviewed evidence of the different levels of progress of pupils on eight model programmes. They concluded that, 'Inclusive programming effects are relatively unimpressive for most students with disabilities especially in view of the extraordinary resources available to many of these model programmes' (p.177).

The effects on progress of pre-school children including progress in verbal and perceptual skills of three forms of provision (special school, integrated provision and mainstream classes) were compared by Mills, Cole, Jenkins and Dale (1998). Higher functioning children were found to benefit more from integrated provision while relatively lower functioning children benefited more from special school classes or mainstream.

Student's perceptions across eight studies have been analysed, indicating social benefits to students in a general education setting compared to when they were withdrawn in a resource room (Vaughan and Klinger, 1998). But students preferred to receive support in the resource room rather than in their usual classes because they considered they were able to concentrate better and older students believed they learnt more.

On a more general level, some studies have taken an overview of evalua-tions of inclusion (eg Sebba and Sachdev, 1997; Tilstone, Florian and Rose, 1998). Others have considered particular types of SEN. For example a review of the educational achievement of deaf children maintains that several studies indicate higher achievement for deaf pupils in mainstream schools but that many studies had not taken account of confounding factors (Powers, Gregory and Thoutenhoofd, 1999).

It has been concluded that such overviews and, reviews, 'cannot be said to be ringing endorsements' and 'fail to provide clear evidence for the benefits of inclusion' (Lindsay, 2003, p.6).

Optimal education

(a) Reasons to question inclusion

It will be seen that there are several reasons to question inclusion:

- Pupils in special schools are not oppressed or excluded by virtue of being educated there. The real oppression faced by pupils in special schools is the threat of political correctness forcing an inclusion agenda and denying them the opportunity of a good education.
- The 'equal opportunity' for a child to be educated in a mainstream school might not be an equal opportunity for the child to receive a good education or for the child to be 'included' in the usual meaning of the term.
- Concern about the supposed subordination of children in special schools can be balanced against the fact that children can be marginalised in ordinary schools. However, all schools might take better account of the views of their students and involve them more in decisions affecting their lives.
- Many pupils identified as having SEN speak highly of their special school. Others who have attended special schools have gone on to continue to participate in society, appearing to benefit from the special educational provision that accompanied the identification.
- The inflation of 'rights' is leading to their devaluation. Rights have become simply a way of expressing wants. They are sometimes contradictory. The 'right' to attend mainstream is rejected by numerous parents.
- It is not fair to base one's treatment of pupils on irrelevant criteria. Inclusion itself is an unfair policy involving a refusal to discriminate on seemingly relevant criteria.
- Overviews and reviews of inclusion do not give ringing endorsements.

(b) What is optimal education?

An alternative to inclusion, 'optimal education' involves mainstream and special schools working together in a joint enterprise of optimising the attainment, achievement, progress and personal development of pupils with SEN. Such an approach would be assisted by a range of provision including, as well as mainstream and special schools, pupil referral units, units based in mainstream schools and learning resource rooms to which pupils are withdrawn from time to time.

But there is crucial difference between this and inclusion. There would be no underlying assumption that special schools are revolving doors or temporary holding stations for pupils with SEN whose real place is in a mainstream classroom. Good special schools (in terms of encouraging pupil's achievement, progress and development) would be valued as much as good mainstream schools.

Decisions would be made whether a pupil would be taught exclusively in special or mainstream school or (when a pupil is taught in both) for what proportion of time and for what subjects and aspects of the curriculum. But these would be based on the progress that the pupil makes in the particular school(s) in the particular areas. In other words, the judgement would be educational, taking into account a pupil's progress.

Academic progress and personal and social development would be assessed and monitored using increasingly shared forms of assessment, for example, National Curriculum assessments or Performance (P) scales and their more detailed variations. Judgements would be made by teachers and others in consultation with parents and pupils about the best 'package' of education for a particular pupil given the strengths and weaknesses of the provision at the present time in the respective special and mainstream school. This would inform such provision as outreach, in reach, consultancy and training provided by special schools.

If this led to the pupil being taught exclusively or almost exclusively in a special school for long periods of time, there would be no suggestion that the pupil was somehow being deprived.

(c) How optimal education meets problems faced by inclusion

Optimal education meets the problems faced by the inclusion agenda as follows:

- Pupils in special schools, far from joining the vast swathes of society that increasingly incredibly are being seen as 'oppressed', will be seen as liberated from the grip of political correctness and enjoying the best possible education. Extreme social views that a typical teacher can, if she only works hard enough at removing 'barriers', teach any and every child successfully will be rejected.
- Equal opportunities claims will be seen as relating to the equal opportunity to have the best education rather than the equal opportunity to attend a mainstream school or a special school.
- Schools will continue to be careful that account is taken of pupils' views and that they are involved in decisions affecting their lives.

- The weak moral claims that inclusionists have tried to support will be left behind. All the 'rights', 'wants' and claims for particular versions of 'social justice' will be secondary to the desire to enable pupils with SEN to learn, develop and achieve as well as they can.
- Providing a good education will be seen as the greatest mark of respect that a parent and teacher can show towards a child.
- The empirical evidence will be recognised to be weak in support of inclusion in many instances. But it will be reviewed in relation to particular pupils, at particular times, in particular circumstances, in certain schools, using particular interventions, involving certain types of SEN and certain levels of severity. These particularities will inform the day-to-day co-operation of mainstream and special schools as the achievement, progress, and development of pupils is monitored and evaluated.

England is in a privileged position compared with many countries in the extent and range of data that it has on the attainment, achievement and progress of pupils, including, increasingly, pupils with SEN. This enables LEAs and schools more and more to be able to examine the progress of pupils with different types of SEN in mainstream and in special schools.

For example Hampshire LEA uses such data on pupils with different types of SEN in its mainstream and special schools going back several years (Farrell, 2004, pp.41–2). Therefore parents and others can make judgements about the progress their child is likely to make. If they regard schools as mainly about education and are concerned about what their child will learn at school, such information is not just of passing interest. It is of central importance.

Thinking points

Readers may wish to consider:
- the various ways in which a special school can respond to the weakness in the arguments for inclusion and emphasise the school's strengths and its positive role in a range of local provision.

Key text

1   Farrell, M. (2005a) *Key Issues in Special Education: Raising Standards of Pupils' Attainment and Achievement* London, Routledge.

This book argues for focusing on improving standards of attainment and achievement and ensuring the personal and social development of pupils with SEN and includes a consideration of curriculum and assessment, target setting, inclusion, funding, and using achievement data to improve provision. Chapter 10 applies these matters to special schools.

Parents' Views

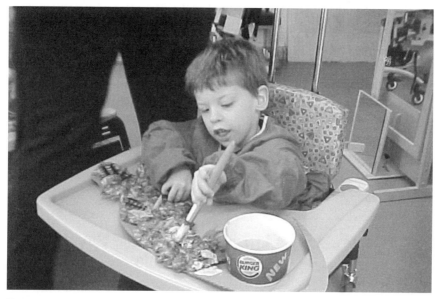

For some parents, 'inclusion' in mainstream school or nursery is remembered with anxiety and education in a special school comes as a welcome improvement. One parent says of her daughter:

When H. was three, it seemed as though we had a child who could do very little except scream and object to most situations. She had attended a mainstream nursery for two short sessions each week. I used to dread taking and picking her up as it highlighted the enormous gap between her and children of the same age and I did not want to hear the feedback from the staff. I was made to feel that I had a child who was beyond help. How things changed when H. started at Brooklands, Reigate. I will never forget picking her up on her first day. I arrived a little early to find the whole school in assembly. As I watched tentatively, I heard H.'s name being called out to receive a certificate for being such a star on her first day at school. I felt such a sense of pride and things just got better from that moment on. I started to think more positively, encouraged by the constructive feedback from staff. The great thing was that H. was nothing unusual to them and they knew exactly how to deal with her.

(personal communication, 2005)

Among 3,000 parents who responded to the consultation for the Special Education Needs 'Green Paper', *Excellence for All Children: Meeting Special Educational Needs* (DfEE, 1997), for every one parent who favoured mainstream school, 20 favoured special school. Naturally, it cannot be assumed that those who expressed their views were a representative sample of all parents but the ratio is at least an indication of the strength of feeling of some parents.

This chapter examines parents' views supportive of special schools. It sets out a selection of parents' views cited in *The Report of the Special Schools Working Group* (DfES, 2003) and presents other parents' views drawing on personal communications.

Parents' views in *The Report of the Special Schools Working Group*

The Report of the Special Schools Working Group (DfES, 2003) included an appendix of the views of parents regarding the future role of special schools (ibid. pp.123–51). This emerged from a request by the Special Schools Working Group to the Council for Disabled Children in 2002 to organise four focus groups for parents and for children and young people. Two parent focus groups took place (in London and in York).

The London group comprised parents who were regional co-ordinators for the national parent association Contact a Family (p.124). Participants came from 15 local authorities across England and two local authorities in Wales. Their children had special educational needs including moderate learning difficulties; dyslexia; attention deficit hyperactivity disorder; behavioural, emotional and social difficulties; autistic spectrum disorders; physical and sensory disabilities and 'learning disabilities' (although it was not made clear what the latter meant) (p.125). Their children attended either ordinary or special schools including residential special schools. The York group was co-ordinated by a parent organisation, Special Families. Several other York-based organisations were represented in the consultation process covering children with 'learning disabilities'; dyslexia; attention deficit hyperactivity disorder; and autistic spectrum disorders. Individual comments and views were also considered from 'a wide range of parents' (p.126).

Some parents expressed satisfaction with their child's mainstream provision, others with their child's special school education. The following summary focuses on what parents valued about special schools, as well as what were perceived as some of the limitations of provision in ordinary schools.

There was a 'widespread perception that the provision of any non-educational services in mainstream schools was becoming increasingly difficult'. Also some parents strongly felt that 'special schools could offer a much less restrictive environment for pupils with health or intimate personal care needs' (p.128). Most parents with children in special schools were satisfied with special healthcare provision (p.142). Among the benefits were, as one parent said, 'the availability of regular health input into special schools' (p.142).

A parent describing the proposed closure of a local special school for pupils with behavioural, emotional and social difficulties referred to parents as 'desperate'. The parent continued, 'their children were excluded before they got to the special school, they found a "safe place" and now they will be on the move again' (p.129).

Parents of children with autistic spectrum disorder were concerned at the variable provision of specialist support in mainstream schools and at parents' 'battles' to get 'high quality provision' associated with residential special schools for children with very challenging behaviour (p.129).

A number of parents had a 'philosophical commitment' to inclusion in a mainstream school, while other parents were 'more pragmatic' (pp.131–2). For the latter, social inclusion of their child in society was a longer-term goal while in the shorter term 'they wanted to identify the school which would offer their child the best possible education' (p.132).

A parent who reported being told by her daughter's mainstream school that the child would not learn a modern foreign language 'because it would be too difficult and would disrupt the class' stated that 'our local moderate learning difficulties school does teach French so "Michelle" would have done better there' (p.133).

Several parents of older pupils identified as having moderate learning difficulties noted that a decade ago their children would have probably been in special schools whereas now 'they were usually in mainstream where some parents felt their needs were often marginalised or misunderstood' (p.133).

Some parents of children with hearing impairments 'felt strongly that separate education was not segregation but a cultural and human right' (p.133).

Parents whose children were educated at a special school were 'generally positive', feeling that their children were offered 'appropriate education' and had access to 'high quality specialist support' (p.133). Most parents had achieved the special school place after 'considerable argument and debate' or appeals to the SEN and Disability Tribunal. Parents who had pupils at residential special school were 'equally satisfied' (p.133). Among the advantages of special schools, parents identified positive expectations; no difficulties in administering medicines; a fully accessible physical environment; better behaviour management; and access to external specialists. One parent stated that in special school, in contrast to ordinary school, there were 'no frowns and meaningful looks about his behaviour, no sudden summonses to the school to hear about his difficult behaviour' (p.134). While some parents mentioned concerns about the small size of special schools, their possible isolation, potential for over-protectiveness and stigma, it seems ironic that, despite the many positive views, a further concern was 'uncertainty about the special school sector's long-term survival' (p.135).

Two parents felt that 'their lives and those of their children had been saved by residential special school placements' (p.138). One parent notes, 'it is probably easier for a residential special school to work as a team – there is a very close 24-hour relationship between pupils and staff at every level' (p.145).

One parents' group highlighted the 'rapid increase' in parents seeking special school placements as their children moved from the primary school sector (p.151).

Regarding shared placements, one parent stated, 'I don't see any point in disrupting my child between two sites unless there is a real programme which benefits him socially and educationally. These arrangements need to be carefully planned so that everybody benefits. Otherwise it is just stressful and confusing for the child' (p.135).

One parent described how she fought to have her son removed from mainstream school to a special school where the school nurse and staff had the time and the confidence to monitor the pattern of his seizures and their impact on his learning (p.136). This enabled the pupil to later return to ordinary school.

The views of parents whose children are educated in special schools

The following section presents a small sample of the views of parents whose children are educated in special schools, indicating some of the features of special school provision that they particularly value. Many of these are taken from personal communications, for example, where parents have written unsolicited letters to the special school that their child attends.

Perceptions about inclusion in terms of the balance of attendance at special and mainstream schools were assessed through the analysis of a questionnaire issued to parents as part of research into parental experiences of special educational provision within one LEA (Wilmot, 2006). The questionnaire, constructed with the help of a parent support group, was issued to all parents with a child attending a shire county special school for pupils with moderate learning difficulties, and returns were anonymous. Positive and negative phrasing of questions was used to detect dissimulation and a range of question formats was employed to discourage the possibility of respondents automatically ticking response boxes.

Of the respondents, 87% of parents believed that decisions about special educational needs were made on political not educational criteria. Some 93% felt that current placement in special school was the best available option and 89% indicated they would prefer their child to stay in a special school for all their lessons. A full 96% of parents stated that they would prefer the pattern of special school provision to stay as it is and 93% did not want to consider alternative placements for their child.

In May 2005, I held a discussion with parents of pupils attending Rectory Paddock School, St Paul's Cray, Orpington, Kent, a school for pupils with severe to profound and multiple learning difficulties. Parents volunteered their views on special schools in general and their school in particular and were asked to give their views on mainstream provision.

J., whose daughter attended the school, said,

Some pupils cannot mix well with other pupils in mainstream schools. They might have behaviour problems or can't be left on their own. They might need a lot of help with feeding. These children benefit from a special school. Any parent who has never visited a special school should just go and visit and see how happy it is. It is a safe environment and the child feels safe too. Closing special school is just about budget cutting. You get lots of staff support and the staff are well trained and it all costs a lot of money.

S., whose son attended Rectory Paddock, stated,

As a parent, it is hard to come to terms with the fact that your child needs to go to a special school and every parent experiences a period of denial. J. first went to a unit in a mainstream school which offered him a limited amount of integration, but as he got older, this was no longer able to meet his needs – it is hard enough having a child with learning difficulties without the added pressure of fighting for what you want in terms of an education for your child. At Rectory Paddock he has thrived. His communication skills and behaviour have improved way beyond our expectations. The classes are between eight and ten pupils with a high ratio of adult support per child, which creates a workable environment in which our children can develop. To place a child with severe learning difficulties into a mainstream school would not be a practical solution for the child or the school. Our children are by nature demanding and in some cases disruptive. J. has a really short attention span which would make it impossible for him to sit for any length of time. He is not able to read and write appropriately for his age so how could he develop in a class of other ten-year-old children? Our children need to have their own community where they are safe and happy. The special school allows them to develop at their own pace and teaches them valuable life skills – the reality is that this is not possible in the standard state system. Parents considering sending their child to a special school should visit, ask to meet other parents whose children already attend the school and most importantly think about what is best for their own child.

L., whose son aged 13 attends, said,

My son has experienced three different special schools and this was the best one. There are small classes and minimum distractions. There is a lot of work on life skills, not just the National Curriculum. The pupils go on residential trips to help develop independence. There are practicalities – a mainstream school cannot provide all this. In mainstream the facilities are not there for inclusion. The infrastructure is not there. And you don't want to go into a school where you are not welcome. It's harder to include in secondary school – there's a wider gulf. Mainstream schools, particularly secondary, do not seem to welcome severely disabled children or children with severe learning difficulties. In a special school it can be harder to build social contacts after school because of the travel. But you just have to think about the child's needs – like therapies. Are they going to get all that at another place? If you wait until secondary age to look for a special school, you can see all the things they (the child) has missed out on if they had attended a special school earlier and the wasted opportunity. Inclusion does not exist at the moment and I do not want to make my son part of a social experiment.

S., whose daughter attended, said,

We had to fight to get a place at special school – at the SEN Tribunal. My daughter is epileptic so nursing is important. Staff here are passionate about their work. There is more support than in mainstream and you can talk to the staff. The staff do not feel sorry for them (the pupils) and encourage them to work hard. Mainstream cannot provide this sort of medical care and she (daughter) would get lost in mainstream. Mainstream is all about pass rates and exams. We wanted her to get the best education. Having a special school next to a mainstream school might help. But integration works well if it is very short term, say a session a week. If the government had their way and closed any more special schools I'd go to America.

T., another parent, stated,

It might be easier sometimes to include a child in mainstream when they are infants. My son was in a mainstream unit for two and a half years. He is autistic. It was a disaster. He became aggressive – throwing stones in the playground. The staff did not seem to have the knowledge that they have in special school. I don't think they were properly qualified. I remember the headteacher here showing me round. It was completely different. They look past the disabilities. Here (Rectory Paddock) the staff are properly trained and the ethos is very happy. They make learning fun. He (son) has found friends here now.

Contributions in annual reviews indicate the views of parents. For example, a parent whose child attended St Margaret's School, Tadworth, Surrey, stated, 'C's education at St Margaret's School and care at Woodland House (a residential house) is exceptional. C. receives support, help and opportunity to achieve from the moment he wakes in the morning until he falls asleep at night. C. is cared for with dignity and respect in a loving and warm environment. C.'s return to general good health . . . is due to the careful monitoring and management of his medical and care needs' (parents' report and comments, personal communication, 2005). Another parent writes, 'I am extremely happy with St Margaret's. The placement suits her (daughter) very well as demonstrated by her eagerness to get to school and how happy she is when I leave her (there)' (parents report and comments, personal communication, 2003). Yet another comments, 'J. is very happy and contented at school and gets very excited when going to school and the staff do a fantastic job' (parents' report and comments, personal communication, 2005).

The parent of a pupil attending Oak Leigh Gardens, South Tyneside, a school for pupils with severe to profound and multiple learning difficulties, writes in a parents' questionnaire, returned anonymously,

I particularly like the welcoming atmosphere of the school. All the children are very polite and well mannered. Staff clearly have high behavioural expectations of the children. I find all the staff very approachable and they are happy to help and offer suggestions for any problems we may be experiencing . . . Daily comments in the diary let me feel part of my child's day which wouldn't happen without the diary as my son is non-verbal. I am aware of my son's individual education plan and do what I can at home to support my son meeting his targets.

I support the school's view of inclusion, which is based around social activities, although I do not believe the view that it is beneficial to all children to attend mainstream education. I do believe that children between the two sectors should mix, as it is a learning experience for both. Oakleigh supports this view and has managed to locate many mainstream friends for integration opportunities . . . I am pleased it is for all children and not just the most able who get to participate.

(Source: Parents' questionnaire)

A parent of a pupil at New Rush Hall School, Ilford (www.nrhs. redbridge.sch.uk), a co-educational day school for pupils with behavioural, emotional and social difficulties, says of the school, 'Great atmosphere, plenty of facilities for the kids to learn and it's given him (son) a chance.'

Parents of pupils attending Freemantles School in Surrey value the school, as letters received by the school indicate. One parent writes, 'My son, M., was diagnosed at the age of 27 months as being autistic . . . Coming to grips with his diagnosis has been devastating and remains one of the worst things I have experienced. Freemantles have put a feeling of calm, hope and reasons to be optimistic back into our lives. Their dedication and support is truly incredible and I will be forever grateful for their existence.' Another parent states, 'I am writing to thank Freemantles School for educating and caring for our son G. Freemantles is a wonderful, secure, happy environment with knowledgeable staff, supporting children and parents and enabling children to develop their abilities, growing, learning, and having fun with their peers.' Another writes, 'Freemantles is a wholly trusted sanctuary. I know when M. is there he is being challenged to learn, not only to read and write, but equally to know how to get along in society, skills that will, I hope, enable him to lead as fulfilling a life a possible when he leaves them' (Source: letters provided by Freemantles School from parents).

A parent of a pupil attending the Royal School for the Blind, Liverpool, writes (Newsletter 28) about her son's progress:

My son R. joined school last autumn and has attended the pre-school group for four afternoons per week. Since attending the school, he has become significantly more confident with his environment and in his interaction with people. R. enjoys listening to songs in assembly and knows, 'Hold my Hand' very well, at which he smiles and kicks his feet. He has also started to make friends and interact with other children.

Another parent of a pupil at the Royal School for the Blind, Liverpool, also writes (Newsletter 27) about her son's school with great satisfaction:

M's teacher, and her team, have been a great gift for M. All my concerns about him being the least able in the class evaporated completely when I saw the work they've been doing over the past year. He loves music and story telling, both of which he enjoys in abundance in his class. On one visit, I remember joining in with songs, which were illustrated by the most imaginative tactile props . . . There is no doubt in my mind that the staff at the Royal School for the Blind are experts in their field. Their dedication and professionalism contribute to the growth and development of each child . . . This is the first time in M.'s life that he's had his own friends, not friends of the family, not his brother's friends, but friends who value him for who he is. There are some amazing children in M.'s class who have demonstrated an enormous amount of caring support in his first year. He's fortunate to be a welcomed member of a great bunch of people . . . The openness and willingness to communicate that I've experienced from the school has been extremely reassuring . . . I really value the relationship I have with the school.

At Peterhouse School, Southport, parents responding to questionnaires issued as part of the 2004 accreditation process, expressed a range of positive views about the school. These included: 'The school supports all the children who attend and their families with the utmost professionalism and care'; 'Individual needs are assessed thoughtfully and regularly and then addressed with well-planned strategies'; 'The review system is excellent'; 'The staff are superb with the pupils and we feel part of the school – a truly wonderful place'; and 'Expertise in autism is second to none'. Other parents of pupils at the school have independently expressed similar endorsements. One parents wrote to the school, 'We have really struggled with life with (our daughter) over the last six years. We have worried particularly about her education . . . To see all the thought and care and the obvious dedication your staff have for the children is extremely reassuring for us as parents. We feel that (our daughter) is very privileged to attend such a wonderful school and hope that she will be an asset to you.' Another parent wrote to the school when her son reached leaving age, 'T. regards you all as his extended family and friends. He has made fantastic progress during his time at Peterhouse and that is all down to you – your dedication, caring, under-standing and patience. We will never forget how friendly, caring and supportive you have all been.'

Parents recognise the importance of specialist help and accurate assess-ment of special educational needs. Parents whose son attends Brooklands School, Reigate, write, 'Our son was sent to Brooklands School with no language/no diagnosis/severe learning difficulties and very little understand-ing of the world he lived in and within one year of being within this amazing school with its fantastic staff he is now a delightful, happy, confi-dent, bright child with a diagnosis of autistic spectrum disorder. We came to Brooklands School as a family who were completely out of our depth and within a year we received such great degrees of support, reassurance and guidance that we are now able to enjoy our son and he can in turn enjoy his life and the world around him' (letter from parents to author, 2005, personal communication).

Another parent writes of 'the very noticeable advantages of a school specialising in special needs as opposed to a mainstream school with a special needs unit' (personal communication, 2005). Parents notice the high aspirations that good special schools have for their pupils. A father states, 'Our son who has Down's Syndrome has attended a special school since starting the nursery aged two. We have seen him grow in confidence and develop his own personality and sense of humour and independence because of the approach to his education adopted there. In particular, always expecting more of him, giving him choices to make and including the parents in this process so they can support his programme at home' (personal communication, 2005).

Thinking point

Readers may wish to consider:

* the views of parents in support of special schools and how in an LEA area it is assured that parents have a choice of local special school should they wish it.

Key text

1   Farrell, M. (2004) *Special Educational Needs: A Resource for Practitioners* London, Paul Chapman

This book examines various disciplines relating to special education: history, sociology, law, politics, ethics, economics, medicine and psychology, as well as looking at the national, local and school frameworks in which special education operates. Readers may find chapter 4, 'Political Judgements, Inclusion and the Future of Special Schools', of interest.

Pupils' Views

Pupils often notice the improvement in the quality of their education after finding a place in a special school. One pupil said,

> When I moved to the special school, I found I could really do my work. Everything was presented in a way which I understood. Really, there was more time. And more understanding. After my [road traffic] accident, I found it hard to concentrate and I got muddled. I needed help to learn. They gave it to me. I think I will get back to mainstream – college anyway – but I needed to learn how to manage my life again (DfES, 2003b, p.160).

This chapter examines the positive views of some of the pupils attending special schools. It sets out a selection of pupils' views cited in *The Report of the Special Schools Working Group* (DfES, 2003b) and presents other pupils' and ex-pupils' views drawing on personal communications. Finally, I underline the importance of open communication with pupils in special schools.

Pupils' views in *The Report of the Special Schools Working Group*

The Report of the Special Schools Working Group (DfES, 2003b) included an appendix of the views of pupils concerning the future role of special schools (pp.152–70). This emerged from a request by the Special Schools Working Group to the Council for Disabled Children in 2002 to organise four focus groups for parents and for children and young people. Two pupils' focus groups drew on existing membership and facilitators of Triangle (an organisation based in the southeast of England with experience in consulting disabled children and young people on a range of issues) and the Bolton Inclusive Play Project (an inclusive play and leisure service). Participants were aged between 8 and 16 years and their disabilities and special educational needs included sensory disabilities; moderate learning difficulties; autistic spectrum disorder; attention deficit hyperactivity disorder; behavioural, emotional and social difficulties; dyslexia; and 'learning disability'. They attended or had attended ordinary schools, day and residential special schools including hospital schools, and resourced units. Personal communications from other pupils were also included in the report (p.154).

A boy with multiple disabilities following a road accident, who had attended a special school and later transferred to an ordinary school, said, 'they [the special school] made me more independent, they made me start doing things on my own' (p.156).

Pupils who had moved from ordinary school to special day or residential schools were asked what was different about their new schools. Among the responses were:

Friendlier

Nicer, my mum's really pleased that I am here now!

Doesn't get so wound up about the way I behave!

Doesn't make a fuss about my medication

Doesn't worry if I have a seizure, says they can cope all right and it's nothing to worry about

More friends – I can walk to school with them

I get my therapy now, I never got it at 'Y' school (p.157).

The report notes that pupils also expressed positive views about mainstream school if they attended one and points out that 'they were responding positively to schools in which they felt valued, confident and safe, regardless of the sector to which the school in question belonged' (p.158). There were also positive reports about provision in resourced units (eg p.164).

Regarding accreditation, one pupil stated, 'At my special school, we got certificates to show people we could do things. My new [mainstream] school say I can't do exams' (p.159).

One boy was angry that his mainstream school had no private place for individual therapy. He described the embarrassment of 'stripping down in the gym' when other younger children were using it (p.163).

A young man with ADHD said that in his mainstream school 'there is nowhere you can go to wind down, it's so noisy and disturbing somehow. Sometimes all that noise just does your head in' (p.163).

A young woman attending a special school stated, 'You're not a problem because they expect you to be like you are! There are more staff ready to help. When I was in mainstream my mum said I was a pioneer; they had to learn from me! Now I am back in special school to get really independent – next stop college' (p.165).

Some pupils felt that mainstream schools did not have the necessary skills to really listen and respect, for example 'not understanding special communication needs, not allowing sufficient time, not looking at the best way of offering accessible information' (p.167).

Regarding managing any personal assistance or support for health needs, pupils in special schools were 'generally happy with such support and had no complaints' (p.168).

Two pupils at residential special schools felt that, 'distance was no barrier' to family partnerships and told of their pleasure that parents and siblings could come and stay at the school if they wished (p.169).

Two other special school pupils praised their school for its outreach role in the family home and making links with local mainstream schools (p.169).

The report clearly states that, 'Although some literature on pupils' perceptions of education suggests that they may feel special schools to be stigmatising, no negative messages emerged from our focus groups' (p.169).

The views of other pupils and ex-pupils of special schools

Following a discussion of County Council inclusion proposals in 2004, two pupils at Walton Hall, Staffordshire, a special school for pupils with moderate learning difficulties, expressed concerns that pupils were bullied in mainstream schools and are often afraid to ask for help in a mainstream classroom. Both pupils were school representatives and members of the Staffordshire Advisory Body for young people aged 13 to 19 years. Following on from the discussion meeting, the pupils undertook a survey of the views of 62 pupils aged 7 to 13 years attending Walton Hall. The survey was designed, conducted and analysed by the pupils. The survey indicated that 48 pupils had attended mainstream primary schools and 21 had attended mainstream secondary schools, for periods ranging from one to nine years. Asked whether they were happier in their present special school than mainstream, only three pupils said they were not, with 59 stating they were happier in special school. Among the problems reported in connection with mainstream schools were bullying, teasing, not getting enough help, classes being too large, and getting into trouble. Reasons for liking their special school included getting more help, liking the staff, having more friends, being understood, no bullying or teasing, small classes, being able to get examinations, everyone being the same, and having more things to do. Of the 62 pupils surveyed, 55 stated that they would not want to return to mainstream school (survey results available from the school).

Pupils attending New Rush Hall School, Ilford (www.nrhs.redbridge. sch.uk), a co-educational day school for pupils with behavioural, emotional and social difficulties, comment on the help they have received (Source: school's DVD 'Partnership in Practice').

One boy states, 'I think it's a very good school. I think it should be all over the country and all over the world for pupils with behaviour difficulty problems . . . When I'm here with a bunch of boys that's got emotional disabilities, I feel more comfortable and more confident.'

Another pupil says of the staff, 'They don't see you as really naughty children. They see you as normal children but with problems and they help you sort it out.' Another child states, 'I have been going to this school for seven and a half terms. Since I have been here, I have learned to control my anger. The teachers are brilliant and they give us hard work and that's good 'cos you get to learn.' A pupils says, 'I enjoy this school because it's made me improve my handwriting, my reading and my maths . . . Since I've been to New Rush Hall, I've controlled my behaviour and listening to the adults well. I haven't been kicking off.'

A pupil who formerly attended Coxlease School (www.coxleaseschool. co.uk), near Lyndhurst, Hampshire, an independent residential school for pupils aged 9 to 17 years with severe behavioural, emotional and social difficulties, wrote to the school in 2004 as follows:

> I would like to take this opportunity to say thank you for everything Coxlease School has given to me. I arrived at Coxlease School in 1999 with many difficulties that needed addressing. I was very insecure, vulnerable in many ways, a sad little boy with many issues. Due to the great staff force you had working at Coxlease School, many of the issues were addressed and sorted out, helping me to turn into a decent young person. The Care staff helped me with my behaviour, socialising skills, life skills including cooking and many of my home issues. The education staff helped a lot with my behaviour, and education, helping me to achieve well in my GCSE examinations and hopefully I did well. Once again I would like to say a big thank you to the care and education staff as well as to the management and therapy department. I will be looking forward to starting life at College, meeting new people and achieving many things for my life later on.

An ex-pupil of the Mulberry Bush School (www.mulberrybush.oxon. sch.uk), in Standlake, Oxfordshire, a non-maintained residential school providing therapeutic residential care and education for emotionally troubled and vulnerable boys and girls, wrote to the school 20 years after leaving it as follows:

> I attended the Mulberry Bush. I am sure none of the staff I knew are still in attendance (after 20 something years) and the School has undoubtedly changed dramatically. When John Armstrong was headmaster there, he had the practice of reading letters to the children from people who had left. Here's my contribution. I will never forget the life there and the profound impact it had on my life. The love of one teacher in particular who would

read me the *Lord of the Rings* in our 'special time'. I was one of the more problematic of the 36 children as I remember it, who out of a possible seven 'big nights' (being allowed to stay up later) managed to garner one. That was an achievement unto itself. At three and a half, I witnessed my mother beat my sister to death. I was sexually abused by my aunt, though I never told anyone. Later I would endure some of the worst physical abuse describable. I think about the other children of the school and the lives that bring them there. Kids whose only crime was to be born to parents or situations that were at the very least toxic. But life has a way of turning to roses. Today I am happily married, living in the USA with two beautiful children. I am a published author and a successful programmer. As you can imagine, this is a dream come true that I am sure people at the Bush would appreciate. Those of us who survived the brutality of the past will never forget it, but we can rise above it. If I could give the children of my old school a piece of advice it would simply be to have a little hope. Life has so many surprises and no matter how bad it seems things have a way of making things work out for the better. Sitting in front of the big tree in front of the School with people whose names are lost to time, they could never have realised the difference they made. Anyway, I have been wanting to say that for a long time.

(Personal communication from the school, 2005)

The importance of open communication

No one would want to pretend that every pupil educated in every special school in England enjoys every moment of their school career and fulfils every aspiration. Nor would it be credible to think that every pupil who has attended special school looks back on the experience as an adult with unalloyed pleasure. This would be as unrealistic as expecting to find that every pupil, including pupils with SEN, who had attended mainstream school found everything perfect, or assuming that, having left school, he would remember everything with affection.

But the experiences of pupils and ex-pupils of special schools that have been considered earlier indicate that they enjoyed the effects of the school having high aspirations for the pupils. For example there was a perception that they were afforded greater dignity in a special school where there is privacy for individual therapy, certificates to show the students can achieve, and greater efforts to encourage independence.

Enriched social experiences were indicated in comments relating to having more friends, the school not being worried about seizures but being able to cope with them, and being able to understand the pupil's communication needs. Instead of their mainstream experiences of bullying, teasing, not getting enough help, classes being too large, and getting into trouble, pupils considered that in special school they were getting more help, liked staff, had more friends, were understood, had small classes, enjoyed everyone being the same, and had more things to do.

Better preparation for adult life was indicated in statements relating to special schools being able to prepare for independence, staff having more understanding and more time, and being able to get examinations. Indeed in some instances, a special school provided the prospect of having any kind of adult life at all.

None of this suggests that special schools are perfect. Indeed complacency would be the last response such endorsement should evoke. Special schools need to be constantly alert to pupils who may not be getting the most out of their education and it is important that channels of communication are available so that discontents and suggestions as to how provision can be further improved can be expressed, heard and acted upon.

These might include schools council, individual and group counselling, an ethos of listening and responding to pupils throughout the school, strong relationships between pupils and staff and parents, circle time, the involvement of pupils in their education, including individual educational plans and the targets set in them, and many other aspects of school life. Through such means, the school can hear positive responses from pupils as well as negative ones and is in a better position to listen to criticisms and respond accordingly.

Thinking points

Readers may wish to consider:

- how the views of pupils regarding special school can be established, and how positive comments might help maintain good provision while any negative views can inform improvements in special school education;

- whether it would be helpful for special schools to maintain contact with ex-pupils who wish it to gain access to the considered adult views of their former pupils.

Key text

1   Department for Education and Skills (2003b) *The Report of the Special Schools Working Group* London, DfES. Appendix D: 'The Future of the Special School: Report of the Consultation with Parents and Young People's Focus Group' is especially interesting.

LEAs and Their Support of Special Schools

While in the name of inclusion, some LEAs appear to be reducing the numbers of pupils in special schools without sufficient reference to the quality of education they receive, other LEAs support special schools well.

An LEA and a special school working together can enable flexibility in approach as shown in the example of Blaenau-Gwent.

Blaenau-Gwent LEA

Blaenau-Gwent LEA, a relatively small authority, has worked closely with its one special school, Beaufort/Pen-Y-Cwm School, Ebbw Vale, a day school for 70 pupils aged 3 to 19 years with severe or profound and multiple learning difficulties. The school has developed an outreach role, by placing some of its pupils in mainstream schools for part of the curriculum and by supporting 22 pupils with severe learning difficulties (SLD) who remain on the roll of mainstream schools.

The LEA has encouraged the establishment of dual roll placements whereby a pupil is registered at their local mainstream school and the special school. Negotiations between the two schools have resulted in the amount of time the pupil spends at either school being gradually adjusted until the pupil spends the amount of time appropriate to their needs at either school. The regular contact with parents has indicated strongly that they are happy with this flexible approach.

Special schools, of course, work within a wider context of provision, such as specially resourced mainstream schools that provide for pupils with SEN. Also, where there is to be restructuring, it is done through consultation, with the role of the special schools being clear to avoid suspicions that restructuring is a euphemism for culling. The good work of special schools can also be acknowledged publicly. The example of Reading LEA below illustrates some of these points.

Reading LEA

Regarding Reading LEA in Berkshire, Reading's Learning Support Service, which supports mainstream schools and pupils, involves staff working with six designated Resourced Schools and peripatetic staff working within the remaining schools. Four Resourced Schools started in 2005 are for pupils with moderate learning difficulties (MLD) and speech and language delay. Two further Resourced Schools are planned for 2006. The peripatetic service works with pupils and teachers in all mainstream schools offering short-term specific support programmes for particular areas of need. The education department has recruited staff skilled in working with pupils with various learning difficulties and disabilities. A speech and language therapist employed via the health authority works directly with pupils in mainstream schools, focusing on the years around and beyond secondary transfer and working with staff supporting pupils with language impairment and the pupils themselves.

Reading has three special schools: The Avenue (all age), Holy Brook (primary), and Reading Alternative School (secondary) and values them and the skills of their staff, which are publicly acknowledged. Special schools staff are invited to be involved on all the LEAs committees and project boards. They contribute to in-service training and the Education department is seeking to further develop this. Reading offers special school-based and focused training and accredited training as necessary and as requested.

Holy Brook special school was refurbished and extended in 2005. After local consultation, the education department proposed to replace another of its special schools, which has ageing buildings, with a new special school scheduled to open in 2007. This new school will educate pupils having profound and multiple learning difficulties (PMLD) and those with severe autism. There will be changes to admission arrangements for the school to match the pupils attending with the support available in the new school. The LEA does not intend to move any pupils currently attending this school unless their parents wish this. It is expected that all older pupils currently attending will either leave to move into further education or employment, while the other pupils will transfer to the new school. Future pupils will be considered for the new school if they have autism, physical disabilities or PMLD.

A particular interpretation of inclusion may be articulated emphasising that the venue for education is less important than such factors as pupils self-esteem and motivation (not to say achievement and development). From such a perspective the movement of pupils between special and ordinary schools is more likely to be two-way. Where special schools are co-located with mainstream schools such a two-way perspective can be helpful in informing the amount of time a pupil might spend in special or mainstream. Kirklees LEA, for example, has co-located some of its special schools.

Kirklees LEA

Kirklees LEA, West Yorkshire, supports six special schools, educating pupils with various types of SEN including PMLD, SLD and behavioural, emotional and social difficulties (BESD). Kirklees seeks to celebrate diversity, remove barriers to learning and provide equality of opportunity for children from birth to 19 years old, of which 64,000 are in school settings with 670 of these pupils attending a special school. Kirklees LEA sees inclusion as relating to how young people feel about themselves and how they are motivated to participate in school and in wider society. Therefore, in determining how 'included' a pupils is, the LEA believes that where a child attends school and whether it is a special or mainstream school is less important than the experiences he has. The LEA recognise the key role of special schools in ensuring that children with complex and severe SEN are enabled to be, and to feel, included. Special schools are regarded by the LEA as an important part in the jigsaw, which covers a range of provision to meet a range of needs.

A reorganisation of Kirklees special schools took place in 2006–7, seeking to ensure that the schools have fit-for-purpose, high-quality accommodation and facilities appropriate to the needs of the pupils and staff who work in them. The LEA invested £4 million in the financial year 2004–5 on general work in reorganisation and some specific work on special schools and plan to spend a further £25 million for three new special schools. Reorganisation led to half of the LEA's special schools being co-located on a campus with one or more mainstream schools. The special schools and mainstream schools that merged under reorganisation already worked together to develop shared curriculum planning and to share subject-specialist teaching expertise. All of the special schools have key partners with whom they work, enabling them to develop a role as a key training provider in the local group of schools and on the campus. The dedicated training facilities also support work with parents, community groups and bring together the wide range of agencies supporting the work of the special schools. Special schools educating pupils with similar types of SEN work together and develop and apply best practice.

LEA monitoring indicates high-quality teaching and learning in Kirklees special schools characterised by teachers' strong understanding of the curriculum and the subject, alongside a very good knowledge of the children and of their development and the implications of this for their learning. Small teaching groups assist more individualised learning, and support staff make a strong contribution. The LEA has provided accredited training for support staff over a number of years.

The LEA supports Kirklees special schools in developing research into teaching methods and practice to support children with SEN, for example developing action research and experimental approaches. Many staff, highly skilled in observation, make careful assessments and use imaginative and accessible approaches to recording children's progress. Some special schools in Kirklees offer outreach support to mainstream schools, for example through advice from teaching and support staff or the provision of teaching and learning resources and equipment, and there is scope for this work to develop further.

Links with partner schools facilitate the inclusion of children with SEN, involving for example paired activities with groups and classes in mainstream schools and special schools. Movement both ways is encouraged. Such links have also included joint visits or work with visitors in the arts, sports and personal and social development. Where mainstream schools are specifically resourced to meet particular SEN, special schools perform a key role in linking to and supporting such provision.

Kirklees LEA's special schools are challenged in their monitoring and self-evaluation in the same way as all other schools and all the special schools have been involved in an LEA–school scheduled discussion intended to validate the school's own evaluation of its strengths and areas for development. These discussions take into account the school improvement plan, the school's completion of Ofsted self-evaluation forms and progress since the last inspection. As a result each special school has identified a number of priorities for the current year's work. Support is brokered with consultants from the LEA or from LEA subject-specialist school improvement officers. During the year, in parallel with mainstream schools, the special school's link advisor visits to provide advice, guidance and support or to check progress. This could include classroom observation, work scrutiny or discussion with pupils and staff. Progress with these priorities is reviewed towards the end of the school year.

In addition to the existing continuing professional development programme, a specific programme is developing for school leaders, all staff and governors in order to support inclusion. Among issues covered are the development of special schools for the twenty-first century, the management of change, curriculum leadership, classroom practice and positive behaviour management.

Another role for the LEA is to channel funding, such as that for government initiatives, effectively, involving special schools fully. The LEA may produce materials to encourage liaison between special and mainstream school staff and can also work with SEN regional partnership projects, as illustrated in the example below on the Wirral.

Wirral LEA

Wirral LEA, Wirral, in Merseyside has 12 special schools: Clare Mount, Elleray Park, Foxfield, Gillbrook, Hayfield, Kilgarth, The Lyndale School, Meadowside, Orrets Meadow, Stanley, and Wirral Hospital School. The twelfth, a new school for pupils aged 11 to 16 years plus with BESD opened in 2005. This school has a Key Stage 3 learning support unit, which performs a similar function to a pupil referral unit and works closely with the newly reorganised pupil referral unit for Key Stage 4 pupils.

The LEA made a successful bid for government funding for over £350,000 to develop extra curricular and out-of-hours activities. In 2005, this involved eight of the special schools as well as mainstream schools. In the DfES-funded primary learning networks, special schools are actively involved and play a key role. Wirral LEA promoted the formation of these groups in primary schools so that each should contain a primary special school. These networks aim to ensure that every teacher in every primary school has the opportunity to work within a group of schools, strengthening pupil learning and implementing effective continuing professional development programmes.

In liaison with the LEA, special schools have been developing inclusion projects that meet the target of developing themselves into specialist schools. From 2002 to 2005, over £90,000 was dedicated to this initiative from the LEAs Standards Fund. There are two principle aims to the initiative. The first is to develop closer links between special schools and mainstream schools with the intention of increasing the capacity of mainstream schools to meet the more diverse range of pupils' teaching and learning needs. Special schools already provide a wide range of advice, support and training opportunities for mainstream colleagues. The second aim is to support full-time and part-time reintegration activities for pupils with statements of SEN. The part-time reintegration activities involve individual pupils and groups of children being given the opportunity to work alongside pupils in mainstream settings through engaging in a broad range of activities at which they can succeed.

A number of special schools have been involved in the LEA's Inclusion Training Programme focusing on developing the ability of mainstream colleagues to increase their skills in working with pupils with different 'types' of SEN. This may involve for example working with pupils with autistic spectrum disorder (ASD), SLD, MLD, and speech, language and communication needs. Orrets Meadow School, for pupils with SLD, offers service level agreements to mainstream schools as part of developing its specialist role.

The local authority has developed challenging School Self-Evaluation materials for mainstream and special schools that focus on 'How effective is our school?' The production of these materials has involved liaison activities with both special and mainstream school colleagues. Wirral authority offers to all schools the opportunity to share its good inclusive practices by applying for a local authority inclusion award. This award is accredited by LEA officers, headteachers and special education needs co-ordinators from mainstream and special schools working together to accredit good and very good inclusive practice across the full spectrum of educational settings.

A further development, 'Managing Inclusive Classrooms – A Web Based SEN Training Audit' is a Greater Merseyside Regional SEN Partnership project to gather information about the existing and future training needs of all staff in relation to inclusion, SEN and disability. This web-based training audit form enables schools and local authorities closely to match their training provision to each school's particular in-service training needs. It also provides a vehicle for local authorities to organise joint training activities to high- and low-priority training needs. This information is collated at three separate levels: school, LEA and regionally. The Greater Merseyside SEN Partnership will be able to negotiate with training providers and broker for the delivery of a wide range of courses at a variety of levels including awareness, refresher and extended.

LEAs may seek to balance plans to educate a larger proportion of pupils in mainstream schools with the necessity to maintain sufficient places in special schools and arranging better access to special schools for short-term or part-time placements where these are suitable.

The potential for the co-location of special and ordinary schools for allowing day-to-day contact, dual placements of pupils and joint training of special and mainstream staff may be developed.

West Sussex LEA

In West Sussex the 13 special schools are at the heart of local developments relating to the LEA's priorities of supporting educational inclusion in its broadest sense and achieving the highest possible attainments for all pupils, including pupils with SEN. New forms of specialist provision are being planned for special schools, for example for pupils with ASD or PMLD. The local authority is seeking to balance making provision for a larger proportion of pupils in mainstream schools and retaining sufficient places in special schools while arranging greater access to special schools for part-time and short-term placements. The county council strives to consult carefully with parents, headteachers and governors of special and mainstream schools and others in developing its strategies and in implementing its reorganisation proposals. The Parent Partnership Service has played a key role in sustaining effective communication with parents and partner organisations through regular newsletters about the major reorganisations of special school provision in both Crawley and on the south coast.

In the period 2000 to 2005, the demand for special school places in the Worthing and Shoreham areas was greater than the number of places available. Following a successful bid to the government under the national Targeted Capital Fund, the county council was able to commit funds to the building of a new purpose-built secondary special school, Oak Grove College in Worthing. This was part of the reorganisation of the three previous special schools on the south coast in terms of the range of pupil needs, the age range and location. Highdown previously educated pupils with SLD or PMLD aged 2 to 19 years. The new secondary special school was designated for up to 240 pupils with a range of learning difficulties and aged 11 to 19 years. Herons Dale School in Shoreham and Palatine School in Worthing, formerly for pupils with MLD aged 5 to 16, are being refurbished and will cater for a full range of learning needs for pupils aged 3 to 11 years.

This move towards age-phased special schools was supported by the co-location of each of the three special schools with a mainstream school. The reorganisation has enabled the county council to provide improved special school accommodation in the Worthing and Shoreham-by-Sea areas for up to 460 pupils, a net increase of up to 45 places on what was previously available in the south of the county. In part, this re-provision seeks to respond to the increasing number of pupils with ASD. It also took advantage of the one-off opportunities presented by the 44% decline in pupil numbers in the county's residential school for pupils with MLD since 1995/96. The closure of this school in July 2004 gave savings, which were recycled to support the reorganisation of the three special schools on the south coast.

The local special schools contribute to multi-agency working, for instance by working with mainstream colleagues in their particular 'family group' of schools and partner agencies. The special schools are a source of expertise, advice and development for mainstream staff. For example, special school staff have for a number of years worked closely with their mainstream colleagues to support the inclusion of children with SEN.

Special school managers and governors have worked closely with LEA officers and others in a multi-agency steering group developing the proposals for the reorganisation implemented in 2005. A similar arrangement applied to the planning, and opening in Easter 2004, of two purpose-built replacement special schools in Crawley (Manor Green Primary and Manor Green College). These reorganised schools operate under similar inclusion principles to the three new south coast special schools.

The development of inclusive practices and opportunities for staff and pupils in mainstream and special schools have been aided by the existing co-location of several special and mainstream schools in West Sussex. This allows for day-to-day contact, dual placements of pupils and joint training of special and mainstream staff. These have been supported by the county council through the Standards Fund and through two years' of funding devolved to local family groups of schools for collaborative educational inclusion projects. A targeted reintegration scheme also funds the carefully planned return to mainstream school of special school pupils whose teachers and parents agree that they are ready to make this move following good progress in their special school placement.

A programme of reviews may be adopted, to systematically examine and develop provision, including provision in special schools and involving headteachers and staff, to seek agreement on current and future needs of pupils and the implications for special schools. This is one of the approaches in Surrey as indicated below.

Surrey LEA

Surrey County Council provides service for a large, diverse shire county in which there are 178,000 pupils, 5,400 of whom are supported in their education via a statement of SEN. Many pupils with statements are successfully educated and supported in mainstream schools. Surrey also has 25 special schools, including schools with residential facilities, to provide for pupils with more complex SEN, and these schools are recognised by the LEA as giving invaluable education and support.

Developments within special schools are carried out under Surrey's SEN Strategic Plan 2004–8 which contains an SEN policy and an action plan to improve provision for children and young people with SEN. Surrey has adopted a programme of reviews, based on themes to systematically examine and develop provision, including provision in special schools. Past reviews have covered: BESD; learning difficulties; SLD and ASD; and language and communication. Each review has involved headteachers and staff, enabling Surrey to achieve a common understanding on the present and future needs of pupils and the arrangements in the special school sector that should be put in place.

Surrey has committed itself to reorganising sectors within its special school community and to large-scale capital projects to support the development of provision. Plans include: the renewed focus on secondary provision for pupils with learning difficulties and the phasing out of Key Stage 2 provision. These changes began in 2004. Schools are undergoing building improvements to enable these changes, which involve the schools supporting associated specialisms such as learning difficulties and ASD. Schools for pupils with learning difficulties will also be enabled to operate outreach services to mainstream schools from September 2006. From September 2005, the two schools for pupils with learning difficulties that specialise in learning difficulties and ASD offered an outreach service based on that specialism.

There are also plans to rebuild a school for pupils with SLD and a school for pupils with complex ASD. The latter will have an attached residential facility managed by Surrey County Council's Children's Service. The development of both school projects has been a joint approach from both officers and school staff. Surrey has two special schools for pupils with complex ASD and both have operated successful outreach services for a number of years in partnership with the local authority.

Major developments have also taken place in special schools for pupils with BESD and social difficulties with new curriculum being developed and residential facilities being completed in 2005.

In 2005, officers and schools began working together to produce a new funding formula. This is led by officers, but makes full use of information provided by schools and has a regular consultation process in place to ensure that schools are kept fully engaged. Over a number of years a dedicated team in the LEA has supported special schools by providing training in areas such as restraint (with a progressive programme of training) and staff skills. Dedicated social work and educational psychologist time has also been attached to schools that educate pupils with BESD to enhance the support and experience of the pupils attending such schools. A link SEN consultant works with special schools (and mainstream schools). Surrey Children's Services has a number of staff who support special schools including a Service Development Manager and the senior educational psychologist responsible for county-wide SEN projects.

The role of special schools can be agreed and articulated in strategic documents variously named, for example a 'Strategy for Special Provision'. Funding may be provided to enable special and mainstream schools to work together in 'inclusion networks' with supportive training.

Birmingham LEA

In 2005, Birmingham educated 1.5% of the school population in 28 special schools and provided statements of SEN for 3%. The LEA has developed a definition of inclusion in partnership with others, acknowledging that promoting inclusion should be an aspiration for the whole education service with *all* individuals, mainstream and special schools, early years settings and services within Birmingham understanding the contribution that they make. Inclusion is seen as a process entitling all learners to a broad, relevant and stimulating curriculum in the environment that will have the greatest impact on their learning and where they are able to learn, play and develop alongside each other within their local community of schools. Every learning environment should meet the needs of learners, families and communities and have access to effective and efficient resources to enable this to happen. Birmingham LEA has sought to ensure, in developing its plans and policies, all its schools including special schools play a key role. The LEAs successful special schools are considered to have an important contribution to make in educating some children directly within the special school and in sharing specialist skills and knowledge to support the education of pupils in mainstream schools. The process for developing the role of special schools has been the Birmingham 'Strategy for Special Provision'. This sets out a vision for the future role of special schools and resource bases as part of local communities of schools, within an overarching framework of inclusion to provide for children in a range of local schools including special schools.

In recent years, the Birmingham 'Standards for Inclusion and Success for Everyone Under 5' have been revised and are being used by 80% of schools and early years settings across the city for self-evaluation of inclusive school development and review. Evaluations indicate that teachers feel the effectiveness of their teaching and confidence in managing pupils with SEN has increased as a result of input from support services. Funding has been provided for over 255 special and mainstream schools working together in 'Inclusion Networks' to share successes, develop their skills and build the capacity of mainstream schools and settings to educate proportionately more pupils with SEN. Training has been provided for over 460 schools on new legislation and inclusion, and training opportunities are available in an Inclusion Training Directory. Plans have been agreed for all 28 special schools to join with mainstream schools in local areas, including building developments. All special secondary schools are included in 'Building

Schools for the Future' plans. The LEA has mapped the issues and local programmes for change, ensuring that all partners are included and involved. The approach emphasises outcomes, in line with the Children Act, and the development of Children's Services to ensure that local placements are available to meet the local need and that local communities of schools work together to meet needs; and to develop flexible and responsive special provision.

While moving towards the development of Children's Services, the LEA's expected outcomes are: children playing, learning and developing alongside each other in their local communities of schools; parents with confidence that their children's needs will be met quickly and effectively throughout their education and as they move into adult life; and those working in schools, early years settings and other front-line services having the skills, confidence and support to remove barriers to learning. The LEA's work with special schools, its commissioning strategy for buying places, and the development of the outreach services, is evaluated against these outcomes and indicators.

The LEA is seeking to have more of its children and young people being maintained within local communities and consequently seeks to reduce the number of pupils placed in independent or non-maintained schools outside the LEA. The LEA's special schools are central to ensuing that the provision is in place, and delivered to the highest standards. In the years 2002 to 2005 all inspected special schools were good or better in terms of leadership and management. Many have done an excellent job in providing education and maximising the potential of children with SEN.

From 2005, the LEA has been reviewing the role of leaders, developing the training opportunities for leadership teams of special schools and schools with resource bases including induction, preparation for headship, vision, ethos and attitudes regarding inclusion, links with 'Leading for Inclusion' and other mainstream leadership programmes. The LEA is seeking to encourage special school links with mainstream schools and how it can share best practice. It is developing data and self-evaluation tools to see how schools get better at using data systematically to monitor the progress of individual pupils, understand who is at risk of underachievement and plan interventions on the basis of their data and on evidence of what works. The aim is to encourage special schools and resource bases to use data on outcomes to evaluate provision systematically and support other schools to do this. The LEA is building on the use of the 'Standards for Inclusion' and evidence to support self-evaluation.

Birmingham is sharing good practice in special schools and resource bases in using Performance levels to assess pupils, plan curriculum/learning opportunities and monitor progress. In line with the workforce strategy, the LEA is organising teaching assistants to fulfil new roles and supporting teachers to plan and adapt curriculum and teaching methods to meet all pupils' needs. The schools work in partnership groups, networks and collegiate structures, to develop their roles and curriculum to meet local needs. This is linked to 'Building Schools for the Future' planning and the development of extended school clusters, the aim being to deliver integrated working in multi-agency teams and ensure children receive the best local provision.

Where an LEA has a good data system, it can indicate to schools, parents and others the progress of pupils with different types of SEN in mainstream or special schools, as illustrated below. (See also the model diagram on p.62.)

Hampshire LEA

Hampshire County Council's proposals for special schools include the aim to develop and support the effective implementation of their SEN policy, inclusion policy and behaviour support policies. Hampshire special schools are seen as an integral part of the school community, working with mainstream schools, other children's services and voluntary organisations. The strategy includes a commitment that any school reorganisation involving specialist provision will ensure that 'change is led by the principle of quality of provision rather than a focus on organisation, accommodation and structure' (Hampshire County Council SEN Strategy).

One of the ways Hampshire LEA supports its 28 special schools is through a commitment to their continuation and development as schools valued in their own right, not as revolving doors or holding stations awaiting mainstream school transformation. The LEA operates a system of data collection and mathematical modelling drawing on assessments of pupils using Performance (P) scales and National Curriculum levels. Pupils having statements of SEN whether they attend a mainstream unit or special school are tested annually. Data are also collected for many pupils with statements that are taught in mainstream primary school classrooms using P scales. All schools having pupils with statements of SEN were invited to participate. From 2005 the software system was available for mainstream primary schools with five or more pupils having statements and for mainstream secondary schools with ten or more pupils having statements. All schools are provided with paper copies of the returns and the analysis. This allows comparisons to be made between the progress of pupils with similar types of SEN educated in mainstream and special schools. Since 2000, the LEA collates this information, producing mathematically modelled trend lines for the whole county. The LEA has provided exemplars across subjects for P scales 1 to 8 and the judgements of teachers about P levels are moderated. The LEA provides software free of charge to schools to generate comparisons between county data and individual school performance data.

The progress data, in standardised form, are published, giving the schools and parents the opportunity to see how a particular pupil progressed in relation to an average child of the same age with the same type of SEN. Other analyses are also used, for example schools are able to see whether their pupils in Key Stage 1 with SEN progressed more in say English than was typical across the county.

This information is available separately for pupils with moderate or severe learning difficulties. The information is available in each of the categories of SEN with an ability to examine progress expectations for, say, children with moderate or severe learning difficulties and autistic spectrum disorder. It is more difficult to extend the approach to some other types of SEN such as autism; behavioural, emotional and social difficulties; or speech and language difficulties – either because of wide discrepancies in performance levels or owing to the small number of pupils involved. While it is more difficult to secure the validity of the data for these smaller groups, such data do exist and are shared with schools for their consideration. For each of the areas of SEN, trends are indicated for subsections of the P scales: personal, social, health and citizenship education (attention; independent organisational skills; interacting); mathematics (shape, space and measure; using and applying mathematics); English (listening; speaking; writing; reading).

From 2005, data also became available for information and communications technology (six aspects) and for science (four aspects).

For each area of SEN, for example for severe learning difficulties, trend lines are produced for each pupil scoring at specified levels. These are the levels at which: only the lowest 5% score; only the lowest 25% score; 50% of the pupils score; only the highest 25% score; only the highest 5% score. The attainment of pupils aged four through 18 years old are indicated by these trend lines.

An individual pupil's starting point in a particular year can be identified, for example, P scale level 1 in Reception, and the trend line of best fit can be identified. This can then inform subsequent targets and for judging added value above the county trend, for individual pupils or for groups of pupils in mainstream or special schools. The data can be analysed by gender or ethnicity and in other ways to explore the differential progress of groups. The priority has been to examine individual, class, year group, Key Stage, SEN groups, and school cohorts.

Vitally, the data can be used to judge the relative progress of pupils in mainstream and special schools allowing LEA officers, schools and parents to make evidence-based judgements about the cost benefits of inclusion. The information allows schools to see clearly their progress and performance and to understand where they need to focus to sustain improvements. (For an example of how a particular special school in Hampshire, Riverside School for pupils with moderate learning difficulties, uses P scales and National Curriculum assessment for school target setting, see Farrell, 2004, pp.42–3.)

Thinking points

Readers may wish to consider, with reference to a particular LEA:
- what policies and procedures are in place to support special schools; and
- what steps could be taken to further enhance their role.

Key text

The 'key text' for this chapter will depend on the local authority area in which the reader lives. I suggest obtaining and scrutinising the LEA policy documents relating to SEN and judging the degree to which they support special schools, perhaps using the LEA checklist in the conclusion section of this book.

Strategy for developing the role of special schools in Hampshire Specialist Learning and Support Centre Model (SEN)

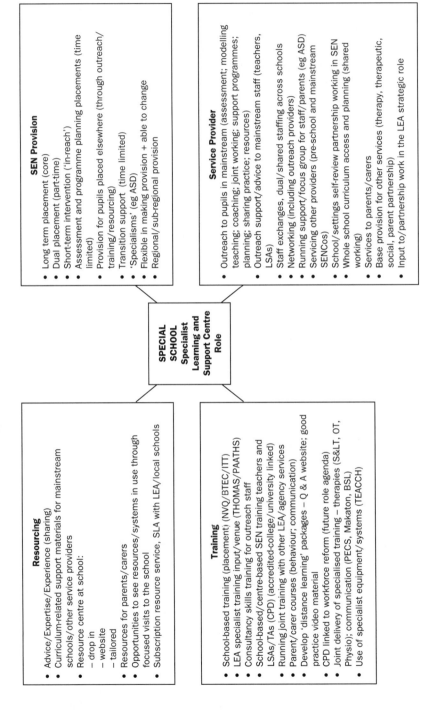

SEN Provision

- Long term placement (core)
- Dual placement (part-time)
- Short-term intervention ('in-reach')
- Assessment and programme planning placements (time limited)
- Provision for pupils placed elsewhere (through outreach/ training/resourcing)
- Transition support (time limited)
- 'Specialisms' (eg ASD)
- Flexible in making provision + able to change
- Regional/sub-regional provision

Service Provider

- Outreach to pupils in mainstream (assessment; modelling teaching; coaching; joint working; support programmes; planning; sharing practice; resources)
- Outreach support/advice to mainstream staff (teachers, LSAs)
- Staff exchanges, dual/shared staffing across schools
- Networking (including outreach providers)
- Running support/focus group for staff/parents (eg ASD)
- Servicing other providers (pre-school and mainstream SENCos)
- School/settings self-review partnership working in SEN
- Whole school curriculum access and planning (shared working)
- Services to parents/carers
- Base provision for other services (therapy, therapeutic, social, parent partnership)
- Input to/partnership work in the LEA strategic role

SPECIAL SCHOOL Specialist Learning and Support Centre Role

Resourcing

- Advice/Expertise/Experience (sharing)
- Curriculum-related support materials for mainstream schools/other service providers
- Resource centre at school:
  - drop in
  - website
  - tailored
- Resources for parents/carers
- Opportunities to see resources/systems in use through focused visits to the school
- Subscription resource service, SLA with LEA/local schools

Training

- School-based training (placement) (NVQ/BTEC/ITT)
- LEA specialist training input/venue (THOMAS/PAATHS)
- Consultancy skills training for outreach staff
- School-based/centre-based SEN training teachers and LSAs/TAs (CPD) (accredited-college/university linked)
- Running joint training with other LEA/agency services
- Parent/carer courses (behaviour; communication)
- Develop 'distance learning' packages – Q & A website; good practice video material
- CPD linked to workforce reform (future role agenda)
- Joint delivery of specialised training – therapies (S&LT, OT, Physio); communication (PECS, Makaton, BSL)
- Use of specialist equipment/systems (TEACCH)

6

Pedagogy 1: BESD and Cognitive Difficulties

In the *Special Educational Needs Code of Practice* (DfES, 2001a) and the guidance, *Data Collection by Type of Special Educational Needs* (DfES, 2003a) the main types of SEN are indicated. Elsewhere (Farrell, 2006a, 2006b, 2006c, 2006d, 2006e) I have described approaches to teaching learning that are considered effective with pupils experiencing different types of SEN, given of course that it cannot be assumed that any individual pupil has only one type of SEN. Related to this are the broader areas of SEN:

- behavioural, social and emotional difficulties;
- cognitive difficulties (moderate, severe and profound and multiple learning difficulties; specific learning difficulties);
- communication and interaction difficulties (including autistic spectrum disorder); and
- sensory impairments and physical disabilities.

In this chapter, I briefly outline, in relation to behavioural, emotional and social difficulties (BESD) and cognitive difficulties, some approaches to teaching and learning and provide examples of special schools where some of these are in place. The subsequent chapter considers communication and interaction difficulties and sensory impairments and physical disabilities.

Behavioural, emotional and social difficulties

The education of pupils with BESD can be understood in terms of the broad underpinning approaches related to them:

- systemic
- behavioural
- cognitive and
- psychodynamic.

Interventions typical of a systemic approach are a framework that helps ensure that the school environment and other factors are examined carefully before 'within child' explanations of BESD are assumed, such as group work, circle time, circle of friends, family therapy, and home–school liaison (Farrell, 2006a, chapter 2).

A cognitive perspective gives rise to interventions such as developing cognitive aspects of emotional literacy; seeking to create more positive self-attributions through for example the technique of 'reframing'; anxiety management and self-talk; and specialist interventions such as cognitive therapy (Farrell, 2006a, chapter 3).

A behavioural approach may involve programmes and schedules of reinforcement; techniques such as time out, fading, desensitisation, and modelling. Among vehicles for behavioural interventions are contracts, token economy, and social skills training (Farrell, 2006a, chapter 4).

Psychodynamic approaches include therapies such as play, music, art, drama, and movement therapy; nurture groups; counselling, to the extent that it has a psychodynamic underpinning; and, more tangentially, developing aspects of the curriculum that encourage communication or the release of emotions (Farrell, 2006a, chapter 5).

A distinctive pedagogy is emerging for pupils with attention deficit hyperactivity disorder (ADHD) drawing on more general approaches to BESD especially cognitive and behavioural perspectives and other strategies. These include providing an environment that is structured, with stimulating learning tasks and minimum disruptions; allowing optimum breaks in classroom work; and, if appropriate, using bio-feedback devices to help the pupil recognise feelings such as frustration and anger at an early stage and deal with them (Farrell, 2006a, chapter 6).

Special schools may draw on several approaches as in Chelfham Mill School, Devon, below.

Chelfham Mill School

Set in 60 acres of countryside, with woodland and a trout stream, Chelfham Mill School, Devon (www.chelfhammillschool.co.uk), is an independent residential school for 48 boys aged 7 to 16 years with BESD including attention deficit hyperactivity disorder. It has particular expertise in providing for boys whose behaviour may be bizarre and children who have been sexually abused. The school has facilities for boys to stay for 52 weeks per year as necessary.

While its provision is underpinned by a cognitive-behavioural approach involving token economy and other methods using praise, rewards, and privileges, the school also provides an eclectic range of therapies including art and play therapy, counselling and psychotherapy. The promotion of self-esteem is given a high priority.

The token economy is ongoing throughout the day in both the classroom and in the residential setting. It is designed to engage the pupils' imagination and themes, which may last for months or over a year, are agreed in consultation with pupils. For example, a theme might involve behaviour being reinforced and recognised by a picture of a car representing a pupil being progressively moved round a 'racing track'. Points are exchanged for privileges or tangible rewards such as special trips to a trading post shop. A personal education, care and therapy plan is developed for each pupil each term, which details assessments and interventions for the pupil.

As part of its outreach approach, Chelfham Mill School operates a 'contract to succeed in mainstream' which offers an intensive course of learning social skills, emotional literacy, anger management, impulsivity control and carefully focused objective-based teaching aimed at enabling a boy to return to mainstream in a relatively short time. The approach involves the school negotiating a pre-agreed timescale with the LEA in which the boy lives.

Other schools, while not closing out different approaches, are known for a particular perspective. The provision at the Mulberry Bush School, Oxfordshire, is predominantly psychodynamic (see below).

The Mulberry Bush School

The Mulberry Bush School (www.mulberrybush.oxon.sch.uk), in Standlake, Oxfordshire, a non-maintained residential school founded by child psychotherapist Barbara Dockar-Drysdale, provides therapeutic residential care and education for 36 emotionally troubled and vulnerable boys and girls aged 5 to 12 years. The school has been based on its current site since 1948. The children, while of average and above average intelligence, have severe emotional damage owing to the accumulation of adverse experiences in infancy and early childhood.

The school works on the essentially psychotherapeutic principle that the children have missed the 'building blocks' of nurturing experiences and seeks to offer them the opportunity to re-experience caring and clear relationships with adults and other children. Among the ways the adults do this is through 'planned environment therapy', using opportunities associated with group living to give the child clear expectations, routines and rules about how to live and get on with others. Education, typified by energetic teaching in small groups, is seen as in itself therapeutic in the sense that success in learning contributes to raising the child's self-esteem.

The staffing structure involves a team of residential therapists; a team of teachers; members of the psychotherapy team (a head of psychotherapy, a child and adolescent psychotherapist and an art therapist); and a family team working with parents through telephone contact and home visits and with other agencies. All new members of staff have weekly induction training in their first year, entitlement to individual supervision, access to supportive team meetings, and consultation with the school's therapeutic advisor. After the first year there is an internal training programme covering a range of issues across childcare and education, supported by 12 study days per year. Staff are also able to apply for training grants to support their continued learning away from the school.

Moderate, severe and profound and multiple learning difficulties

For pupils with moderate, severe or profound and multiple learning difficulties, there are differences in approach with areas of overlap. One of the clearest features distinguishing provision is curriculum and assessment level: for pupils with moderate learning difficulty (MLD) this reflects their greater difficulty than peers in acquiring basic literacy and numeracy skills and in understanding concepts (eg DfES, 2003a, p.3). For pupils with severe learning difficulties (SLD) the curriculum and assessment level is indicated by the learner's attainment being in the range of performance indicators (P scales) P4 to 8 for most of the pupil's school career (eg DfES, 2003a, pp.3–4). With regard to pupils having profound and multiple learning difficulties (PMLD), attainments are likely to remain in the range of P scale 1 to 4 throughout their school careers (eg DfES, 2003a, p.4).

For pupils with MLD, the curriculum tends to be securely subject-based. Teaching and learning includes interventions for literacy such as reading intervention; using concrete and visual apparatus; ensuring relevance to everyday life; providing opportunities for exploratory learning and investigation; and ensuring lessons have a suitable pace. Also, to the extent that pupils with MLD experience 'additional' communication and language difficulties and 'additional' behavioural, emotional and social difficulties, provision takes account of these (Farrell, 2006b, chapter 2).

The work of Alfriston School, Buckinghamshire, and that of Sutton School, Dudley, illustrates some of these features in the examples below.

Alfriston School, Buckinghamshire

Alfriston School, Buckinghamshire, is a county day and boarding special school for 128 girls aged 11 to 18 with moderate learning difficulties, many also having behavioural, emotional and social difficulties or minor physical disability or sensory impairment. A few pupils have severe learning difficulties. It has extensive grounds, gardens and a netball court.

The school curriculum is subject-based. There are five year groups arranged according to the pupil's age and these are the groups for some teaching while for core subjects the pupils are set. Accreditation includes GCSEs, Certificate of Educational Achievement and Associated Examining Board

---

Achievement tests. Careers education and guidance includes the use of computer-based assessment programmes aimed at helping pupils discover likes and dislikes in terms of career interests. Among the strengths of the school are its personal, social, health and citizenship education and pastoral support. The post-16 department involves work on citizenship, community, home management, personal care, and preparation for working life and developing and improving basic literacy.

Sutton School, Dudley

Sutton School, Dudley, is a purpose-built day school for 120 pupils aged 11 to 16 years who have moderate learning difficulties and as the school prospectus states, 'whose needs cannot be adequately be met in mainstream schools'. School facilities include two science laboratories, art room, design and technology workshop, food technology room, information and communications technology suite, modern library and fully equipped music room.

The organisation of teaching in the school capitalises on these facilities. Each child has a class tutor responsible for registration, Record of Achievement sessions, and review and guidance. Specialist subject teachers offer English; mathematics; science; design and technology, including food technology; music; art and design; physical education; history; geography; religious education; personal, social and health education; and information and communications technology.

Curricular strategies for teaching and learning for pupils with SLD may include adapting the National Curriculum, the National Literacy Strategy and the National Numeracy Strategy; using cross-curricular links to reinforce subject understanding and skills; and setting intermediate targets. Assessment may involve small steps assessments such as P scales, B Squared or PIVATs and Records of Achievement. Teaching and learning may draw on multi-sensory approaches; interactive approaches; visual 'input'; augmentative and alternative communication; encouraging communication through music; using information and communications technology to improve access to the curriculum; and developing and using regular routines. Also important are starting with what is familiar and immediate; encouraging choice and decision making; skilfully using questions and developing an understanding of them; capitalising on practical activities; interactive storytelling; developing mobility and co-ordination; and 'room management' (Farrell, 2006b, chapters 3 and 4).

The education of pupils with profound and multiple learning difficulties (PMLD) may include approaches such as providing a curriculum that balances the challenges of responding to a subject-based National Curriculum on the one hand and the developmental learning needs of the pupil with PMLD on the other. Assessment takes account of small steps of progress as well as progress in relation to increasing levels of challenge, improved quality of work, or experience of breadth of activities for example. Also effective are multi-sensory approaches; encouraging communication; linking resources and routines; encouraging pupils to control their surroundings; and building on pupils' interests, aptitudes and achievements. Provision for the medical conditions that often accompany profound learning difficulties is important (Farrell, 2005b, chapter 5).

Many special schools educate pupils who have MLD, learners having SLD, and pupils experiencing PMLD in the same school and a key issue concerns how the curriculum and groupings are arranged to respond to this wide range of attainment. The school may use both generic classes as well as special classes for certain groups, as the two examples below indicate.

St Luke's School, Scunthorpe

St Luke's School, Scunthorpe, is a community co-educational day special school for 97 pupils aged 3 to 11 years who have moderate, severe or profound learning difficulties. About a third of the pupils have medical needs such as epilepsy, physical disability or sensory impairment and a quarter are identified as having autistic spectrum disorder. St Luke's occupies purpose-built premises with a hydrotherapy pool, separate dining and physical education halls, a sensory garden and mobility trails. As well as seven 'generic' classes organised according to the age of pupils, the school has a specialist class for a group of nine pupils with profound and multiple learning difficulties (PMLD) and another specialist class for a group of six pupils with PMLD and autism.

At the foundation stage, the school has developed, in co-operation with the LEA, a modified version of the North Lincolnshire's foundation stage

---

curriculum for all children. Throughout the school, subject leaders have written joint policies and long term plans with colleagues at St Hugh's School (the secondary special school for pupils with similar learning difficulties) to help ensure continuity in the provision. The school has purchased additional teaching support to extend lunchtime activities and this and after school clubs have contributed to the school achieving a PE Active Mark Gold Award.

The headteacher manages four small services: Portage, Child Development Centre Education Unit; Education Preparation Unit; and an Autism Service. The involvement with the first two of these services helps the school to keep track of possible referrals to the school for a place, or for support through outreach work.

A strength of the school is that pupils with severe mobility difficulties benefit from a Movement Opportunities Via Education (MOVE) programme led by a teacher who is a national trainer. There has been substantial investment in training, the purchase of mobility equipment and ensuring that the mobility programmes are integrated effectively into the school day. Consequently, all pupils are reported by the physiotherapist, parents and teachers to maintain appropriate physical development through this intervention and some pupils make significant progress.

William Harvey School

William Harvey School (www.portables.ngfl.gov.uk/dwgodfrey/), Haringey, North London, is a co-educational day school educating 75 pupils aged 4 to 19 years with severe or profound and multiple learning difficulties. Pupils in Key Stages 1 through 4 are taught in the main school building on the same site as a local primary school and another special school (Moselle, for pupils with moderate learning difficulties), while post-16 students use purpose-built premises half a mile away at Waltheof Gardens and link with the College of North East London.

Classes are in mixed ability groups mainly according to age. Teaching and learning, while it is based on the National Curriculum, emphasises approaches that are practical, active and relevant to the pupil's level of development. The core curriculum places great emphasis on communication and on personal, social and health education and citizenship. Multi-disciplinary working including collaboration within curriculum sessions is important. The secondary department particularly highlights self-advocacy and working towards independence through the Youth Award Scheme and Transition Challenge programmes.

The school provides outreach extending to many mainstream primary schools across the borough and loans resources to schools. Opportunities for individual and group integration with pupils attending mainstream schools include a drumming group comprising pupils from William Harvey, Moselle and mainstream primary and secondary schools. The school offers its facilities, such as the soft play room, for individual pupils working from home with a specialist teacher.

Outreach for primary schools also involves providing training for teachers and other staff in their own schools; training as part of initial teacher training involving William Harvey School linking with Middlesex University for one week; information and communications technology advice and access work such as that applying to the use of switches and software; advice on access and buildings; and more general advice for headteachers and special educational needs co-ordinators concerning particular students.

Specific learning difficulties

Specific learning difficulties include dyslexia (literacy difficulties), dyspraxia (difficulties with the co-ordination of movement) and dyscalculia (difficulties with mathematics).

For pupils with dyslexia, interventions include those for supposed underlying difficulties for example, phonological deficit where interventions include raising the learner's phonological awareness in teaching and as necessary providing speech and language therapy. Other provision focuses directly on reading, writing and spelling where, for example, reading interventions may combine phonological training with reading. Still others concentrate on wider issues such as developing metacognitive awareness and building on strengths taking account of learning styles and preferred approaches to learning (Farrell, 2006c, chapters 2 and 3).

Mark College, Somerset

Mark College, Highbridge, in Somerset (www.markcollege.somerset.sch.uk) is a boarding and day approved independent special school for 83 boys aged 11 to 16 years of average or above average ability and with dyslexia. It achieved Beacon status in 1999 and runs teacher training courses in the use of information and communications technology for teaching English and mathematics. The school offers a wide range of sports and activities and has Sports mark award.

All English teaching staff are trained to teach pupils with dyslexia and others are undergoing training. The subject-based curriculum comprises English, mathematics, French, music, history, geography, science, drama, craft and art. In Year 10, GCSE examination courses comprise compulsory English, media studies, mathematics, design and technology, science, information technology and a choice of two other subjects. There is also a general studies programme and the school also teaches organisation and study skills. Creative English work is combined with a structured multi-sensory core course aimed at alleviating specific learning difficulties. All pupils are encouraged to develop their information and communications technology skills and there is access to talking computers and personal computers with voice input software. Emphasis is placed on improving self-esteem.

In lessons, with groups of eight or nine students, the school seeks continuously to address problems such as short-term memory, writing speed, reading difficulties and organisation and to respond to the individual learning styles of the boys. For example, all lessons are broken up into sections to aid concentration. Where a pupil experiences speech and language difficulties, extra support is built into his individual programme.

In educating pupils with dyspraxia, interventions include work on areas such as handwriting, physical education and personal, social, health and citizenship education (PSHCE). For handwriting, strategies aim to encourage a correct posture, develop a good pencil grip, and improve hand–eye co-ordination. In physical education, care is taken in structuring activities so that pupils with dyspraxia can participate, for example adapting games so all can participate (eg volley ball with a lighter ball that gives more time to get into position). In PSHCE, social skills may be taught perhaps using behavioural techniques and the pupil's parents may adapt clothing to make dressing and undressing easier (Farrell, 2006c, chapter 4).

Turning to dyscalculia, approaches include drawing on interventions for dyslexia and dyspraxia depending on the nature of the mathematical difficulties and other interventions. The latter include teaching prerequisite skills in classification, number, length, area, volume, weight and position, and movement. General approaches include reducing pupil's anxiety about mathematics and providing rich and varied opportunities to use concrete apparatus (Farrell, 2006c, chapter 5).

Thinking points

Readers may wish to consider:

- the extent to which particular a special school has developed a pedagogy that relates to the main type of SEN of the pupils it educates in relation to BESD and to cognitive difficulties;

- the degree to which the provision takes into account any other SEN that the pupils may have, for example for pupils with MLD.

Key texts

Each of the books below concern particular types of SEN and the provision associated with them. They also cover definitions of the type of SEN, prevalence, and identification and assessment.

1 Farrell, M. (2006a) *The Effective Teacher's Guide to Behavioural, Emotional and Social Difficulties* London, Routledge.

2 Farrell, M. (2006b) *The Effective Teacher's Guide to Moderate, Severe and Profound Learning Difficulties* London, Routledge.

3 Farrell, M. (2006c) *The Effective Teacher's Guide to Dyslexia and Other Specific Learning Difficulties* London, Routledge.

7

Pedagogy 2: Communication and Interaction Difficulties; Sensory Impairment and Physical Disabilities

This chapter considers pedagogy for pupils with communication and interaction difficulties, including autistic spectrum disorder; and for learners having sensory impairment and physical disability and presents examples of special schools educating pupils with these special educational needs.

Communication and interaction difficulties

The education of pupils with communication difficulties may be understood in relation to difficulties with speech, grammar, meaning, the use of language, and language comprehension. In provision for all of these, the role of the speech and language therapist is important.

Difficulties with speech relate to the speech elements of phonology (which concerns speech sounds that convey meaning), phonetics (which relates to articulation) and prosody (such speech features as volume and patterns of intonation). Interventions include the teacher raising the phonological awareness of pupils in lessons, for example asking how the sounds of words break up and blend back together and if pupils know any similar sounding words.

Problems with grammar involve syntax (the rules for making words into sentences) and morphology (grammatical changes to particular words such as making a word plural). Suitable education includes the teacher ensuring that her communication is direct and clear and supporting the development of grammatical utterances through reading and writing activities.

Difficulties with meaning (semantics) may be characterised according to labelling (naming things), packaging (knowing what things can be packaged together under one label, for example that 'dog' applies to creatures of different shapes and sizes), network building (working out how one word relates to another), understanding idioms, understanding grammar and understanding the meaning of relations. Interventions include the use of structured experiences to help securely build an understanding of different labelling words; and analysing and correcting through practical experiences where a pupil is over or under extending a label (this relates to packaging).

Problems with the use of language (pragmatics) may be considered in terms of grammatical sense in language use, and in terms of social and linguistic sense. Examples of appropriate teaching are developing conversational skills and helping the child with difficulties in the social and linguistic sense of communication.

Difficulties with language comprehension involve the roles of attention and grammar in relation to comprehension, while interventions include the modelling of listening behaviour and encouraging pupils' assertiveness to signal lack of understanding school lessons (see Farrell, 2006d, especially chapters 2 through 6).

In Dawn House School provision includes a language-based curriculum and other curriculum features, while Woodsetton School uses the Derbyshire Language Scheme and, like Dawn House School, emphasises close work between speech and language therapists and other staff, as the two examples below indicate.

Dawn House, Nottinghamshire

Dawn House in Mansfield, Nottinghamshire (www.ican.org.uk), is a day and residential co-educational non-maintained school administered by ICAN, a charity that aims to help children communicate. The school educates up to 95 pupils aged 5 to 19 years with complex speech, language and communication difficulties, offering a combination of specialist therapy, education and care.

The school is organised into primary, secondary and further education departments, the latter having strong links with a local college of further education. Older pupils work towards externally accredited awards for academic, sporting and personal achievement including GCSE, NVQ, Entry Level Certificate and the ASDAN Youth Award Scheme. At the same time, the school meets the communication needs of the pupils through a language-based curriculum planned and taught collaboratively by teachers, speech and language therapists, learning support assistants and residential care staff. The complex needs of the pupils are also met through play therapy, occupational therapy, learning mentor support, and a visiting counsellor.

Woodsetton School, Dudley

Woodsetton School, Dudley (www.woodsetton.dudley.gov.uk), educates pupils aged 4 to 11 years having learning and communication difficulties. There is an emphasis on developing communication skills and encouraging positive behaviour. Among the teaching and learning strategies used is precision teaching in which motivation and progress is encouraged through the use of very short tests or 'probes'. Broader targets are set every six weeks. A speech and language therapist gives individual sessions and also works with specialist teaching assistants to provide day-to-day support for communication difficulties. The speech and language therapist and teachers also provide meetings and workshops for parents. All staff are trained in the Derbyshire Language Scheme, a developmental approach that helps record, structure and encourage progress in early communication.

Members of staff are encouraged to develop their skills and achieve higher qualifications. In 2005, of the six teachers in the school, three were advance skills teachers; of the ten qualified teaching assistants eight were trained to be speech and language therapy assistants, three were training to be National Vocational Qualifications (NVQ) assessors and two were on weekly day release training to be teachers. Level 3 NVQ teaching assistants are cover supervisors under the 'remodelling the workforce' scheme.

Links with other schools are two-way. Woodsetton helps support pupils in ordinary primary schools; the assistant headteacher, who is an accredited Derbyshire Language tutor, and the advance skills teachers work for a proportion of time with teachers in local mainstream primary schools. Some pupils from Woodsetton attend local mainstream primary schools for some sessions while pupils from other schools including local special schools attend Woodsetton for certain sessions if it is considered it will help their progress. The school's active playground approach combines opportunities for physical activities and clubs supervised by lunchtime supervisors and by play leaders. In 2004, the school achieved an Active Mark Gold Award.

The particular provision for pupils with autism and autistic spectrum disorder seeks to take account of the triad of impairments associated with the condition in terms of social isolation, communication difficulties and insistence on sameness. Interventions include an approach often known as Teaching and Education of Autistic Children and Communication Handicap (TEACCH) but which is also referred to as 'Structured Teaching' – an approach emphasising visual cues and structure. Other approaches are the Lovaas programme, which uses behavioural methods to teach skills and reduce unwanted behaviour, and intensive interaction, which draws on techniques relating to early parent–child interaction so the adult acts as though the child's actions were invested with communicative meaning and follows what the child does to eventually encourage communication.

Musical interaction therapy seeks to develop the pupil's ability to enjoy the company of others and his understanding of how to interact and communicate. Signing systems for communication may be used. The Picture Exchange Communication System (PECS) may be used to help children using pictures to request things or activities from others. Social stories can be used to help the pupil understand their social environment and to know how to behave suitably in it.

Also important are managing challenging behaviour if it occurs; managing transitions; and teachers and others learning to use speech optimally (Farrell, 2006d, chapter 7). The examples of Freemantles School and Peterhouse School below illustrate some of these features.

Freemantles School, Surrey

Freemantles School, Surrey, is a co-educational school for pupils with autistic spectrum disorder that is in the process of changing from primary age provision to educating pupils aged 4 to 19 years. Pupils' attainment ranges from age average in school subject terms to attainment associated with severe learning difficulty. Freemantles strives to work very closely with parents.

The curriculum, based on the National Curriculum, includes specific programmes and individual work tailored according to particular difficulties in learning. Within the school some pupils may require individual working. Among the strategies used by the school are the TEACCH approach and the PECS, which are both integral to the curriculum. The school uses social stories, and a variety of behavioural strategies support learning. Some groups follow a sensory curriculum including the use of Intensive Interaction. Some pupils attend mainstream school for a number of sessions per week, supported by staff from Freemantles.

Peterhouse School, Southport

Peterhouse School, Southport (www.autisminitiatives.org), a non-maintained day and residential school for 48 pupils aged 5 to 19 years with autistic spectrum disorder, is administered by 'Autism Initiatives' (formerly the Liverpool and Lancashire Autistic Society). The school offers weekly, termly, and 52-week residential provision. A Family Liaison Officer facilitates links between parents, the school and other agencies.

Teaching methods are eclectic and include a high level of structure and a visual approach to learning as reflected in the use of TEACCH and PECS. Manual signing (Signalong) is used as well as symbols, photographs, objects of reference and the written word, depending on the individual pupil.

The Expressive Arts Department incorporates practice within music, art, physical education and sensory skills. Another strength of the school is the teaching of communication skills (including literacy, social interaction and thinking skills) in which teachers, teaching assistants and speech and language therapists work closely together to assess and provide for pupils' learning requirements. For pupils who are residential, both day and care staff implement communication work as part of the 24-hour approach, with guidance from the speech and language therapist.

Sensory impairment and physical disability

Sensory impairment refers to visual impairment, hearing impairment and deafblindness. Provision for pupils with visual impairment includes low vision devices and suitable lighting (reading stands, spectacles, magnifying equipment, for example); Braille or Moon (a tactile medium base on a simplified raised line adaptation of the Roman print alphabet); hands on experiences and enabling pupils to gain rapid and efficient access to information; and training in mobility and orientation (Farrell, 2006e chapter 2).

The education of pupils with hearing impairment may encompass special attention being paid to communication and literacy and a particular school may have a preference for an oral/aural; total communication; or a sign bilingualism approach. In mathematics, an important focus is the language of mathematics, and placing sufficient emphasis on teaching young children to count in school taking care to avoid confusions that might arise between counting and signing (Farrell, 2006e, chapter 3).

For learners who are deafblind, special attention is given to communication, for example using approaches such as hand over hand work (where the adult moves the pupil's hands slowly and sensitively to show him how to do something); resonance work (which involves the adult reflecting back to the child's movements or vocalisations) and co-creative communication (which emphasises the relationship between the child and the 'communication partner'). Also important are gaining information about the world, and mobility (Farrell, 2006e, chapter 4).

The two examples below provide indications of provision for pupils with hearing impairment and communication disorders; and visual impairment and deafblindness.

The Royal School for the Deaf and Communication Disorders, Stockport

The Royal School for the Deaf and Communication Disorders (RSDCD) Stockport (www.rdsmanchester.org), is a day and residential, co-educational school and college for pupils/students aged 7 to 21 years with severe communication difficulties (such as no or very limited oral language) and complex learning difficulties. Because of the very specialist nature of the provision, pupils are admitted from all over the British Isles. Residential provision ranges from weekly to 52-week per year boarding. An assessment centre provides assessments for pupils who are referred by local authorities as well as ongoing assessments of pupils already educated at RSDCD.

The school uses a total communication approach incorporating sign, speech, symbols (including the Picture Exchange Communication System), and objects of reference, photographs and real objects. There is also a strong emphasis on independence and life skills. It comprises three departments each having a different curriculum and communication emphasis: deaf/severe learning difficulties support; autism support (which offers a low arousal approach through optimising visual and auditory stimuli for learning); and multi-sensory support (including an emphasis on communication, mobility and self-help skills and having an interactive multi-sensory room, a light stimulation room, and information and communications technology adaptations). The college part of the provision is organised into similar departments.

The 250 staff include teachers, residential care staff, an educational psychologist, speech and language therapists, audiologists, a home–school link worker, a physiotherapist, an occupational therapist, a musician in residence and medical staff. An induction and a continuing professional development programme enables a range of training qualifications to be offered including NVQ level 3 in Caring for Children and Young People (Council for Awards in Children's Care and Education), British Sign Language level 1 (Council for the Advancement of Communication with Deaf People) and management training accredited by the British Institute of Learning Disabilities.

The Royal School for the Blind, Liverpool

The Royal School for the Blind, Liverpool (www.rsblind.org.uk), was only the second school of its kind in the world (after a school in Paris) when it was established in 1791. A co-educational non-maintained school for up to 66 pupils aged 2 to 19 years with a visual impairment and additional disabilities, including deafblindness, the school has 14 weekly residential places. All teaching staff have the additional qualification in teaching children with visual impairments and some have additional qualifications in learning difficulties, hearing impairment and teaching children who are deafblind.

Teaching programmes are developed using either low vision or non-visual methods to encourage pupils to develop tactile skills and any residual vision. Print is enhanced by visual aids and some pupils use either Braille or Moon to read. To help develop early literacy skills, a 'Moon room' has been created in which there are a variety of Moon activities. Other facilities include a light room, a soft play area, hydropool and sensory gardens.

In the early years a total communication approach is used, involving speech, signing, body cues and objects of reference as appropriate to each child. In the primary school, mobility and self-help skills form a particularly important part of the curriculum. In the senior department, all pupils work within the National Profile of Record of Achievement scheme through which they aim to gain recognised national certificates before leaving school.

Mobility and orientation is important for pupils of all ages and ranges, from early development programmes enabling pupils to explore their environment, to independent travel. The school has its own mobility and orientation department, staffed by two full-time mobility officers. New pupils have a baseline mobility assessment and based on this, guidelines and schemes of work are planned for each pupil. Great care has been given to the environment through, for example, the use of lighting and decoration, contrast, colour and tone to make it helpful to pupils. Mobility staff help pupils form a mental map of their environment by laying tactile and auditory landmarks.

Physical and motor disability and medical conditions

Relationships between medical conditions, physical disability and mobility are suggested in guidance on data collection for types of SEN (DfES, 2003a) which states,

> There are a number of medical conditions associated with physical disability which can impact on mobility. These include cerebral palsy, heart disease, spina bifida and hydrocephalus, and muscular dystrophy. Pupils with physical disability may also have sensory impairments, neurological problems or learning difficulty (p.7).

To take one example, children with spina bifida and hydrocephalus may require mobility aids and a catheter to assist urination and will need physiotherapy and perhaps occupational therapy and speech and language therapy. In personal, health and social development, among the educational implications are making sure facilities are available that enable the pupil to be as little constrained by the condition as practicable. Motor difficulties and spatial problems may lead to challenges with handwriting and number work and a teaching assistant may help with practical tasks or as an amanuensis.

Other conditions that may have educational implications are muscular dystrophy, cerebral palsy, spinal curvatures, limb loss or damage, epilepsy, cystic fibrosis, asthma, and diabetes mellitus (type 1).

While medical conditions do not necessarily imply SEN, medical conditions have to be managed for effective education to take place. The pupil's educational provision should be responsive to changes in the physical and motor abilities of the child and sensitive to the physical, psychological and any other effects of the medical condition. Regarding conditions associated with physical and motor disability, medical conditions also have to be provided for.

Helpful interventions include: adaptations to the environment; flexible routines; curricular emphases such as personal, social and health education; the effective use of equipment and aids; the support of a teaching assistant; speech and language therapy; and programmes to develop and consolidate motor skills including physiotherapy and motor training (Farrell, 2006e, chapter 5).

The examples below describe two schools that educate pupils with physical disabilities, Treloar School, Hampshire, and Fairfields School, Northamptonshire.

Treloar School, Hampshire

Treloar School (www.treloar.org.uk) in Upper Froyle near Alton, Hampshire, is a non-maintained co-educational school for pupils aged 5 to 16 years and having physical disabilities, which provides education, therapy, and pastoral support. Emphasis is placed on encouraging independence. Its 110 boarders and 40 day pupils come from all over Britain and sometimes from abroad and the school offers a wide range of GCSE courses and other qualifications, including Award Scheme Development and Accreditation Network (ASDAN), Entry Level, the National Skills Profile, and Accreditation for Life and Living (ALL). Class sizes are around eight to ten pupils and often less. Each pupil has his or her own personal computer with access to the Internet and their own email address. An occupational therapist and a rehabilitation engineer liaise with the class teacher to ensure that each pupil has the necessary access devices, which can be made in-house if not available commercially.

Among the distinctive provision that Treloar makes is that for developing movement and cognition. Older pupils aged 11 to 13 years may take part in FLAME classes (Function, Language and Movement Education), which combines traditional movement therapy with conductive education. This involves Peto-trained conductors, FLAME group leaders, speech and language therapists, physiotherapists and occupational therapists, teachers, care staff and technical staff working together to help each pupil develop physically and cognitively. FLAME integrates developing physical skills with the academic and social curriculum.

Outside the classroom there is provision for Scouts, Duke of Edinburgh Award Scheme, youth club, sports, drama, disco, cinema, theatre, and shopping trips. Several students compete at national and international level in athletics, swimming and boccia (a form of bowls). An on-site health centre supports students in managing their conditions and there are patient facilities and expertise to support post-operative care plans as well as to provide palliative care for pupils with life-limiting conditions.

The school employs over 300 full-time and part-time staff including occupational therapists, speech and language therapists and physiotherapists, nurses, rehabilitation engineers, an educational psychologist, a dietician, visual and hearing impairment advisors, teachers, learning support assistants, counsellors and a chaplain. There are 28 teachers, 50 learning support staff and 20 therapists and trained assistants.

Sir William Treloar, then Lord Mayor of London, established his hospital and school in Alton in 1908. In recent years, the Trust has spent over £7 million on projects including new residential accommodation and extensive investment in information and communications technology.

Fairfields School, Northampton

Fairfields School (http://atschool.eduweb.co.uk/fairfields/Fairfields_School_ie.htm), Northampton, is an LEA day co-educational special school educating 65 pupils aged 3 to 11 years who have physical difficulties, communication difficulties and associated learning difficulties. Among its awards is an Artsmark Gold Award for performing arts.

An emphasis of the curriculum is the development of self-esteem and physical independence. In the foundation curriculum, a focus is to encourage the children to improve, use and integrate their sensory awareness (visual, auditory, tactile, gustatory, olfactory and kinaesthetic). For all pupils, among their entitlement to the access to the National Curriculum is the art curriculum, used to develop self-confidence, communication and inclusion, involving other schools and agencies. Visiting artists regularly work with pupils and the school holds annual arts weeks and sensory days. It works closely with local artists and theatre companies to enable staff and pupils develop their artistic skills. An experiential curriculum provides pupils with stimulating situations linked to various areas of experience: linguistic and literary; mathematical; scientific; aesthetic and creative; human and social; physical; moral; and human. It often focuses on the processes of learning, where the knowledge content that pupils are expected to acquire is not pre-specified but where conditions are created under which it is expected that pupils will be helped to develop greater autonomy and understanding of the environment. Personal, social and health education is taught in distinctive sessions, through individual work or is integrated into topic work. Pupils' progress is assessed using performance indicators (P scales).

Among its specialist facilities the school has rooms for soft play, music therapy, physiotherapy, speech and language therapy and a multi-sensory room. Communication aids include Makaton manual signing, PECS, Moon, symbols communication books, talking aids and switches.

Fairfields employs three teachers/conductors trained at the Peto Institute in Hungary and other staff members have also received training. Movement groups based on the principles of conductive education are included in the daily timetable. There is also a half-day a week school for parents of young children from ten months to four years old to work on pre-school conductive education. Mainstream pupils and pupils aged over 11 years who have physical difficulties attend Fairfields for weekly sessions. A team of physiotherapists and physiotherapy assistants is based at the school.

Thinking points

Readers may wish to consider:

- the extent to which a particular special school has developed a pedagogy that relates to the main type of SEN of the pupils they educate, with reference to communication and interaction difficulties, sensory impairment, and physical disability;

- the degree to which the provision takes into account any other SEN that the pupils may have.

Key texts

Each of the books below concern particular types of SEN and the provision associated with them.

1   Farrell, M. (2006d) *The Effective Teacher's Guide to Autism and Other Communication Difficulties* London, Routledge.

2   Farrell, M. (2006e) *The Effective Teacher's Guide to Sensory Impairment and Physical Disability* London, Routledge.

Outreach and In-reach

Outreach, in-reach and inclusion

While outreach by a special school can involve providing services for parents, LEA officers and others, this chapter focuses mainly on the interaction between special and mainstream schools. I discuss not only outreach but also 'in-reach' (in which a pupil from a mainstream school attends a special school for a number of sessions) offered by special schools. It should be clear from the outset that if inclusion is about providing for the best education for pupils with SEN it should involve special schools and ordinary schools working more closely together. There should be no hidden agenda of running down numbers of pupils in special schools if it led to poorer achievement and development for pupils. Given this, a special school will be as likely to provide in-reach as it is to supply outreach services. In other words, it would be acceptable if in-reach leads to an increase in the number of pupils being educated in a particular special school if outcomes indicated that this was providing a better education for the children involved.

The range and variety of activities that come under an outreach umbrella include: a 'hot line' provided by a special school to advise mainstream colleagues (funded by a retainer fee and where costs are related to logged calls); speech and language assessments provided by the staff of a special school; and a member of special school staff assessing the success of a mainstream intervention as an independent evaluator. Social language participatory work (eg the Social Use of Language Programme) can involve a special school trainer taking groups of children in a mainstream primary school observed by the teacher and teaching assistants who will later take over.

It is important that a maintained school liaises with the LEA to ensure that there is co-operation rather than competition. Such liaison and consultation is likely to indicate where there are gaps in what the LEA offer for which a special school might provide. Liaison between a special school and local mainstream schools is also important to establish what services mainstream schools consider they require and such consultations can also act as market priming.

Referral procedures should be clear and agreed with the special school, ordinary schools and LEA officers. A common referral pro forma may be developed. One arrangement is to have pupils referred to the LEA where a designated officer will determine which special school might be suitable to provide the required service. This can help avoid overlap of services and special schools competing to support the same children.

Funding ideally should not be short term although this can be used for so called pump priming. Sources include Standards Fund, Beacon funding, the use of advanced skills teachers and contributions from a charity. Longer-term funding is more likely if the special school has consulted with the LEA from an early stage. The LEA for example may agree to fund extra places in a special school in exchange for services such as in-reach or outreach. Other approaches include no cost quid pro quo arrangements between special and ordinary schools. Mainstream schools may also fund services provided by a special school as part of arrangements for network or cluster funding.

An overall strategy should involve the Schools Forum in determining strategy and agreeing funding streams. Careful planning is essential, including financial planning. But in-reach and outreach needs to be integrated into school development planning, not seen as an 'add on' service. Forward planning will include arrangements to deal with the tensions between staff commitments to the special school and increasing commitments to other schools for outreach. Parents and other agencies should be involved and all should be clear about the purpose of the services offered and the expected outcomes.

Outcomes should be clearly determined before services are offered and evaluation of the success of the services will then include the extent to which the outcomes have been achieved. This can also form part of any service level agreement between the special schools and the LEA and ordinary schools. The South West SEN Regional Partnership has developed a self-evaluation framework for outreach providers (www.sw-special.co.uk).

Individual pupils, small groups and whole school developments

Outreach takes various forms. Often, it is linked with inclusion in that, where pupils attending a special school are educated for part of the time in a mainstream school, special school staff may be involved in supporting the pupil(s) and supporting and advising the mainstream staff. Similar approaches may also apply to pupils educated for most or all of the time in mainstream school where extra support and advice is provided by special school staff.

Such support may focus on a pupil or small group of pupils involved in the 'inclusion' or may extend to a whole school remit where special school staff assist senior managers in the mainstream school to improve their provision for pupils with SEN. Related to this broad role are such services as special school staff mentoring a mainstream SENCO through a period of change or support for staff in a mainstream school developing a specially resourced unit. Many outreach activities may be understood in this frame-work of individual pupil/small group support or wider whole school development.

An example of outreach affecting whole school development and indeed structure in both a special and a mainstream school is that of Springhead School, Scarborough, in the example below. This also involves a discrete funded project that is evaluated (the Communication Aid Project).

Springhead School, Scarborough

Springhead School, Scarborough (www.springheadschool.com), a North Yorkshire LEA community co-educational special school, educates 52 pupils aged 3 to 19 years with severe and profound and multiple learning difficulties. Classes have multi-media computers and interactive whiteboards and school facilities include a hydrotherapy pool with a computer-generated sound and light system, a controlled audio-visual environment (CAVE), dark and light room and a therapy room. A physiotherapy service is based in the school, and a speech and language therapist, occupational therapist, school nurse and a consultant paediatrician visit regularly.

The school uses Equals schemes of work and **P** scale **A**ssessment of the National **C**urriculum for **E**quals (PACE) and thorough data analysis and challenging target-setting is deeply embedded in the school's approach. For older pupils, the school also uses Equals 'Moving On' scheme. Teaching and learning is typified by close teamwork between teachers and teaching assistants with an emphasis on learning by doing.

The school supports pupils aged three to four years in the mainstream classroom of the adjacent mainstream primary school and there is also a classroom for Springhead pupils aged five to seven years situated in the mainstream school. A 'buddy' scheme encourages older pupils attending the mainstream primary school to befriend a pupil attending Springhead. On the Springhead school site, their class teacher teaches pupils of primary school age for most of the time. Classes for pupils aged 11 and older are organised increasingly on secondary lines, with pupils moving between teachers. Pupils aged over 16 years spend time at the local college of further education.

Springhead is a North Yorkshire Communication Aid Project Centre and many pupils use communication aids provided by the British Educational Communications and Technology Agency/Communication Aid Project Scheme. The school offers other schools ongoing assessment and provision of technological communication aids for pupils requiring it and provides out-reach work for schools in the Whitby area having pupils with SLD. Ongoing staff training is tightly related to school priorities identified to ensure the school continually improves.

Determining subjects and areas of the curriculum for outreach

Where pupils from a special school attend a mainstream school for part of the week, care needs to be taken about which aspects of the curriculum are involved. Should it be a subject that the pupil particularly enjoys or is good at? Should it be a subject in which all other factors being equal appears easier to organise for pupils with differing levels of prior learning and skill, such as art and design or physical education? For Frank Wise School (example below) factors include subject accessibility and staff support.

Frank Wise School, Banbury

Frank Wise School, Banbury (www.frankwise.oxon.sch.uk), is a Beacon Oxfordshire County Council school for 98 pupils aged 2 to 16 years having severe or profound and multiple learning difficulties. Its facilities include a hydrotherapy pool and a purpose-designed music room and a Countrywide Resource Centre comprising a conference/staff room, staff library and resources room. In nursery classes, children learn through play activities and individualised tasks in priority curriculum areas. Around the age of four years, the children generally transfer to the school's integrated nursery based in local primary school. In the primary section and the secondary section of the school, there are clear aims and frameworks for teaching language and communication skills; PSHCE; intellectual and reasoning skills; humanities; numeracy skills; science; technology skills; and physical development. The curriculum for the secondary section also emphasises the development of life skills. Records of Achievement across the whole school, including photographs, video recordings, copies of pupil's work and other evidence, lead to the National Record of Achievement Scheme. At Key Stage 4, pupils' work is accredited through the AQA Unit Award Scheme.

The school aims to ensure that all its pupils spend at least one session a week attending a mainstream school involved in an accessible subject accompanied by their teacher and classroom support officers. Additionally, arrangements are sometimes made for individual pupils whom the school considers could benefit from additional unaccompanied and targeted curriculum time at a mainstream school. Groups of children from local mainstream schools also participate with some of the pupils at Frank Wise

School in various activities. Lessons are jointly planned and delivered with an agreed curriculum focus, which fits in to both schools' long-term planning and the approach is continually evaluated and developed. Frank Wise School offers support to pupils with SEN in local mainstream schools as well as providing opportunities for increasing mainstream teachers' knowledge and skills concerning pupils with SEN, by such means as establishing joint professional development activities, collaborative working, and sharing resources (eg a school-developed pre-reading scheme).

Learning resources and outreach

Special schools may support pupils through work involving learning resources. This may involve special schools providing advice about suitable resources, providing written materials for mainstream schools, or providing information via an Internet website. It may involve a special school loaning specialist equipment or materials (perhaps with a special school and a mainstream school agreeing to share each other's materials supported by a basic contract to cover loss or damage. The loan of equipment is part of the outreach service of Woodlands School, Plymouth, in the example below.

Woodlands School, Plymouth

Woodlands School Plymouth, a school for pupils aged 2 to 16 years with physical impairments, in liaison with the LEA, provides comprehensive outreach services to up to 40 mainstream schools having pupils with physical disabilities on roll. It is funded by the LEA to the extent of 0.8 of a teaching post so there is no charge to local schools and the school's work complements that of the LEA. The school provides a wide range of services including visits to schools; advice and support on transition planning (for example for a child transferring from primary to secondary school); pupil observations; information about the implications of certain conditions; and loans of equipment. The specialist teacher also manages manual handling trainers who provide manual handling instruction courses to special and ordinary school staff (Newport, 2004, p.6).

Training and outreach

Training provided by special schools may be designed for parents, LEA officers, governors and staff of mainstream schools and others. Special schools may also organise conferences, study days, and courses for teachers, learning support assistants and others; lectures, demonstrations, and workshops. Training may involve guidance for governors in mainstream schools with particular SEN responsibility. It may also involve training for teachers, teaching assistants and others on topics including the use of P scales and their moderation; systems of assessment and data monitoring using information and communications technology; manual handling or behaviour management. Training for parents (of pupils attending either special or mainstream schools) can include workshops for a particular type of SEN with a practical orientation.

Independent and non-maintained schools and outreach

It may be easier for a maintained special school than a non-maintained and independent special school to offer outreach services because of its existing network of LEA schools and the support of LEA officers. Also, where non-maintained and independent special schools are residential, they may be some distance away from towns and cities, making travel to mainstream schools situated there more time-consuming. But this does not preclude non-maintained or independent school providing outreach services as the example below illustrates.

National Institute of Conductive Education, Birmingham

The National Institute of Conductive Education (www.conductive-education.org.uk) Birmingham, opened in 1995 by the charity the Foundation for Conductive Education, comprises a registered co-educational independent school educating 20 pupils aged 3 to 11 years having motor disorders and associated difficulties, and a separate Parent and Child Service for children aged from birth to three years. Conductive education, a system of habilitation and rehabilitation, originated in 1945 in Hungary from the work of András Petö, involves encouraging a wide range of activities, has manual, psychological and social elements, and uses 'verbal mediation', rhythm and song.

Set in parkland, the school was designed and custom built. Pupils, who attend full or part-time, follow an individualised programme focusing on the development of movement skills. The Foundation Stage curriculum and the National Curriculum, including the national strategies for numeracy and literacy, are integrated with the conductive curriculum. Specialist teachers teach mathematics, English and science, while other subjects are taught through topics. Individual programmes concentrate on movement and physical skills and include targets for self-care, physical independence and speech and communication. Detailed assessment of each child's academic, physical, social and personal development is used to set targets for improvement.

The Institute is a training centre for student conductors, offering degree-level training comprising practical training alongside qualified specialist instructors, known as 'conductors', and theoretical education. The Institute supports staff wishing to gain qualified teaching status through the Graduate Teacher Training Programme. Outreach services provided by Institute staff include sessional services for particular conditions such as dyspraxia, early intervention for children aged three to seven years, consultancy and staff training. A National Library of Conductive Education is situated at the Institute.

The range of in-reach offered by special schools

If outreach can be varied and wide ranging, so is in-reach. It can involve emotional literacy group sessions in special school for pupils from local mainstream schools as early intervention; the provision of a day nursery for local pupils who do not have SEN by a residential school; or the dual placement of pupils. Teachers from mainstream schools may visit a special school to observe and discuss a particular approach, later modelling it in their own school observed by the special school teacher. Mainstream staff may shadow special school staff in teaching, administration roles, or meetings. Highbury School, West Yorkshire, is developing both outreach and in-reach or 'reverse inclusion' as it calls it, as indicated in the example below.

Highbury School West Yorkshire

Highbury School, West Yorkshire, is a generic special school in the Metropolitan Borough of Calderdale, West Yorkshire, for 41 pupils aged 3 through 11 years having moderate, severe or profound learning difficulties and pupils with autistic spectrum disorder.

The school is organised into five classes: two classes, which currently follow the Foundation Stage, and three working on a differentiated National Curriculum. The school uses the Foundation Profile, the EQUALS scheme of work and some special 'Highbury' schemes of work for curriculum structure and assessment. Each class is staffed with one teacher and two support assistants and in addition, a number of support assistants support particular pupils on a one-to-one basis.

Strengths of the curriculum include the varied and stimulating ideas used within the Foundation Stage to enable pupils of all abilities to access the curriculum; and in the upper school the imaginative use of resources to illustrate subjects in a meaningful way. Music is used to develop communication and great emphasis is placed on the sensory curriculum.

Among the school's inclusion work are that several pupils attend sessions at the local primary school; some pupils from the local primary school attend Highbury for literacy and numeracy sessions; a class from Highbury attend the local school for physical education; and 15 pupils from mainstream join Highbury pupils for sporting activity sessions each week. Highbury is committed to 'reverse inclusion' or 'in-reach' which started as an experiment between Highbury and its link mainstream school when two pupils from mainstream attended Highbury for literacy and numeracy, which gave them the opportunity to progress better in the smaller groups and helped them to gain confidence. This has become an established link and Highbury receives a growing number of enquiries from other schools and parents.

Thinking point

Readers may wish to consider:

- how procedures can be put in place to ensure that special school can provide outreach, in-reach, training and consultancy without lowering the standards of attainment and achievement of pupils educated in the special school.

Key text

1   Newport, F. (2004) *Outreach Support from Special Schools* Taunton, South West SEN Regional Partnership.

Within the southwest region, this report considers the extent and variety of outreach support in the maintained sector; the impact on special schools; funding outreach; overall strategy; partnership with other schools and agencies and with the non-maintained and independent sector; and dual placements. The South West SEN Regional Partnership has also developed a 'Self Evaluation Framework for Outreach Providers' (www.sw-special.co.uk).

Other Issues

Having so far considered pedagogy and outreach and in-reach as issues relating to special schools, the present chapter suggests further themes and issues, some of them also relating to pedagogy. These include: the response of the special school to varied special educational needs; its choices of assessment and accreditation; multi-professional working; parent relationships; and improving pupils' communication.

The variety of SEN for which special schools provide

Where schools have pupils with moderate, and severe and profound, and multiple learning difficulties, or two of these types of learning difficulty, the curriculum and grouping can be organised in various ways. The school may teach these groups predominantly separately enabling it perhaps more easily to provide a curriculum and pedagogy focused on the type of SEN. Or the school may educate the pupils predominantly together with high pupil: staff ratios enabling staff to provide as necessary for pupils working at different levels of the curriculum and in different ways. Or there may be flexible groupings with pupils being educated separately some of the time (for example pupils with MLD and SLD may be taught in 'setted' literacy and numeracy classes) and together for some sessions.

Where such a flexible approach is used, the progress of pupils (including personal, social and emotional development) can be monitored to ensure a sort of optimal education within the special school. In this respect, such approaches mirror the monitoring and evaluation of links between mainstream and special schools where pupils attending a special school may attend certain sessions in a mainstream school in which they can participate well and therefore learn and develop. Similarly, where pupils have autism, they may be taught for all, none or part of the curriculum with other pupils in the special school who do not have autism.

Where areas in which special schools' work appears to be changing, for example the apparent increase in the number of pupils considered to have autistic spectrum disorder, it is important that special schools adapt and ensure that staff training, pedagogy and resources reflect the changing population of pupils. The accreditation of schools by the National Autistic Society is an example of encouragement along these lines.

The example below illustrates one approach to flexible groupings (sometimes called 'clever grouping') for pupils with different types of SEN and how this is complemented by a well-conceived curriculum and specialist teaching approaches.

Montacute School, Dorset

Montacute School, Dorset, is a day foundation special school educating 75 pupils aged 2 to 18 years having severe or profound and multiple learning difficulties, in the unitary authority of Poole. The school is organised into lower and upper schools, and pupils with profound and multiple learning difficulties or medical needs have access to a supported learning class base in which they are educated for part of the week. Also, while pupils with PMLD and autism are included there are specialist bases and staff that support them as required. Montacute was awarded Beacon status in 2000. A home–school communication policy has been developed in consultation with parents, and newsletters, a weekly parents' group meeting and a parents and friends association help communication. The school council meets twice a term. Members of staff are trainers in several approaches, including Positive Behaviour Management, Moving and Handling, signing, and in the foundation degree for teaching assistants.

The curriculum is envisaged as foundation, core and enrichment curricula. The Montacute Foundation Curriculum, laying the basis of later subject learning, relates to the earliest stages of learning and is concerned with the development of sensory, physical, early communication and social skills, with teaching activities being broken into small steps.

The core curriculum areas form the central part of the curriculum through which the child acquires basic skills, competencies and attitudes important in developing personal autonomy. The areas are personal, social and health education (including in the lower school circle time and in the upper school a modular PSHE programme); English; mathematics (including an emphasis in post-16 classes on functional mathematics); home and community (including food technology, and the use of public facilities); and physical education.

The enrichment curriculum (other National Curriculum subjects mainly taught through topics planned for all classes) comprises science; history and geography; design and technology; the creative arts (art, music and drama); religious education; sex education as part of PSHE provision; and educational visits and residential experiences. Information and communications technology supports learning across all areas of the curriculum. The post-16 provision includes team enterprise activities involving the production of items such as handmade paper, candles and handicraft items.

Specialist teaching approaches draw on the principles of small steps teaching and, as appropriate, for pupils with autistic spectrum disorder the TEACCH approach. The Derbyshire Language Scheme and Intensive Interaction are used and texture classification has been introduced to help with feeding skills. Augmented communication systems include communication passports, objects of reference, cueing, the Picture Exchange Communication System (PECS), Signalong manual signing, and communication aids.

Links with local mainstream schools include pupils from mainstream having work experience placements at Montacute, a playgroup held at Montacute each morning for local pre-school children offering shared play with the school's reception class, and joint projects such as in music or drama undertaken with children from local first, middle and secondary schools. Montacute provides support to other special and to mainstream schools in curriculum and assessment, specialist provision, inclusion, and leadership and management; for example, advice relating to curriculum access for pupils with autistic spectrum disorder and support for developing behaviour assessments and strategies. Opportunities for pupils in the lower school include pupils attending sessions in a mainstream school near Montacute or local to the child's home.

Refining the curriculum

Within a special school, the curriculum may be refined and linked to suitable assessment to help ensure that pupils are working at a level and in a way that encourages achievement and development. The example below indicates such developments in a school for pupils with a wide range of learning difficulties.

Barrs Court School, Hereford

Barrs Court School (www.barrscourt.hereford.sch.uk) Hereford, a maintained day school in Herefordshire LEA, educates 56 pupils aged 11 to 19 years with moderate, severe, or profound learning difficulties who may also have behavioural, emotional and social difficulties, autistic spectrum disorder or multiple sensory impairment (deafblindness). The school is organised into three classes at Key Stage 3 (ages 11 to 14 years); one class at Key Stage 4 (14 to 16 years); and two classes for further education (16 to 19 years).

A strength of the school is the extensive range of specialist curricula, based on frameworks of diagnostic assessment criteria supported by corresponding teaching activities. These are able to inform Individual Education Plan (IEP) targets and help differentiate the entitlement National Curriculum because each diagnostic criterion has been linked to P scale performance descriptors. The early thinking skills curriculum (concerning sensory, perceptual and cognitive development) includes the teaching of functional mathematical skills, and thinking skills within the development of scientific understanding, to underpin the earliest stages of National Curriculum mathematics and science (P levels 1 to 4). The early communication curriculum underpinning English (pre-intentional communication, augmentative communication, and total communication) includes the use of Intensive Interaction, sensory cues, objects of reference, the PECS and Signalong manual signing. Functional communication skills and functional reading and writing are taught. The early mobility curriculum responds to pupils with physical disability ranging from relatively minor difficulties with co-ordination to severe difficulties. Among additional therapeutic activities being built into the mobility curriculum are hipotherapy (an adaptation of Riding for the Disabled designed to strengthen the hips), rebound therapy and conductive education.

The further education curriculum includes team enterprise business experience; developing proficiency in the use of community facilities such as banks and libraries, and independent travel training. 'Transition Pathways', a multi-agency scheme trialled at Barrs Court in 2004, aims to help provide pathways to adulthood for pupils aged between 13 and 25 years, emphasising pupils' self-determination, advocacy and personal aspirations.

Whole school targets for pupils' attainment are set and shared with national organisations including EQUALS and PIVATs so that the rate of progress achieved at the school can be compared with that of similar schools nationwide. Formal accreditation includes the ASDAN Towards Independence programme, the Accreditation for Life and Living Scheme, National Skills Profile, and (in association with local secondary schools and colleges) a limited access NVQ level 1 and occasional GCSE courses.

Assessment and accreditation

The importance of suitable, motivating assessment and accreditation can hardly be overestimated. This includes use of commercial tests; curriculum-related assessments; multiple professional assessments; PIVATs; B Squared; P scales; and EQUALS assessments. Accreditation includes GCSE; Entry Level GCSE; Certificate of Educational Achievement; City and Guilds Adult Literacy and Numeracy, and Number power; OCR Accreditation for Life and Learning; ASDAN Bronze Award, Bronze Challenge, and Silver Challenge; GNVQ; and the National Skills Profile.

The school should be able to clearly justify why their assessment and accreditation was chosen and what alternatives were considered. It should be able to demonstrate that the accreditation is challenging for the pupils as well as providing opportunities for them to show what they can do.

Suitable assessment and accreditation inform robust procedures for target setting, bench-marking and value-added measures. For example, where forms of accreditation may not be very widely used, it is helpful if the school can identify a school using the same accreditation so that basic bench-marking can be explored to help each school perform at its best. Linden Bridge School, Surrey, seeks to provide a range of accreditation for its pupils as indicated below.

Linden Bridge School, Surrey

Linden Bridge School, Surrey (www.linden-bridge.surrey.sch.uk), a day and residential maintained LEA school for pupils having autistic spectrum disorder, is organised into primary (4 to 11 years), secondary (11 to 16) and further education (16 to 19) departments. The curriculum emphasis is on encouraging communication skills and personal and social development and building up strategies to reduce the effect of autism on pupils' everyday lives. The school uses the Treatment and Education of Autistic and Related Communication Handicapped Children (TEACCH) programme – some staff are TEACCH trainers – to establish structure and to foster independent working skills; Makaton manual signing and symbols, and the Picture Exchange Communication System (PECS). The curriculum includes enhanced music, art and personal, social, health and citizenship education. Assessments include the Gilliam Autism Rating Scale and the Childhood Autistic Rating Scale as well as tests of academic attainment.

In the primary department regular 'trialling' meetings are held to exemplify levels and standards of pupils' work. In the secondary department there is an enriched PSHCE curriculum focusing on independence, social interaction skills, sex education, behaviour management, self-advocacy and personal development. Pupils assessed as reaching the necessary level of attainment are entered for Entry level GCSE accreditation (certificates of achievement) and some pupils follow GCSE programmes at local mainstream schools. Alternative accreditation such as Transition Challenge and entry certificates is used to reward achievement and develop key skills. The curriculum for the further education department, which provides a careers programme and work experience, consists of key skills, life skills, vocational skills and personal development; and students work towards certificates such as ASDAN further education award and City and Guilds adult literacy/numeracy.

Multi-professional working

The range of professionals that may be based in or brought together by a special school is wide and includes:

- teachers, including qualified teachers of the deaf and of the blind and mobility teachers;
- 'conductors', teaching assistants and voluntary helpers, and ConneXions advisors;
- arts therapists (music, art, drama and dance/movement therapists); play therapists; psychotherapists;
- physiotherapists; occupational therapists; speech therapists;
- orthotists, prosthetists;
- ophthalmologists;
- medical doctors and nurses; podiatrist/chiropodist;
- audiologists; audiological technicians;
- educational, behavioural and clinical psychologists;
- social workers including residential social workers, educational welfare officers; and
- members of the Child and Adolescent Mental Health Service, LEA behaviour support staff.

Among systems and approaches aided by multi-professional working are the co-ordination of statutory assessment information; joint training for aspects of work that have shared responsibilities; joint assessment of pupils; and shared working, such as that between a teacher and a speech and language therapist. The innovative special school will make the fullest use of the professionals working in it and ensure that joint working is supported by suitable systems and that time is accordingly allocated to staff to work together. For multi-professional working to be practicable, clear lines of communication are necessary and a structure that demarcates responsibility without being too constraining. Rectory Paddock School and Research Unit, Kent, places emphasis on multi-disciplinary working, as illustrated in the example below.

Rectory Paddock School and Research Unit, Kent

Rectory Paddock School and Research Unit, Kent (www.rectorypaddock. bromley.sch.uk), maintained by the London Borough of Bromley, is a purpose-built co-educational special school educating 90 pupils aged 4 to 19 years with severe or profound and multiple learning difficulties. The school is organised into a primary, secondary and a further education department (with a distinctive 14 to 19 curriculum including, for older pupils, link college courses and work experience placements). Accreditation in the senior and further education departments include Moving On, City and Guilds Number Power, Accreditation for Life and Learning, ASDAN Bronze Award and Bronze and Silver Challenge, and the First Aid 3 Cross Award.

Emphasis is placed on multi-disciplinary working between its teachers, nurses, physiotherapists, speech and language therapists, occupational therapist and others. An example of this is multi-disciplinary, dynamic, child-led assessment where a music therapist, speech and language therapist and physiotherapist work contemporaneously to build up a picture, for instance, of a child's opportunities, means and motivation to communicate. While the nature of the activities in the assessment session ranges from unstructured to more structured tasks, each therapist has pre-planned assessment aims, and there is a continuous dialogue between the therapists to reflect and clarify arising issues instantly. The school has written and video recorded evidence of this approach, which is used in sharing information with parents, teachers and others.

The school has its own research unit used to evaluate the curriculum and investigate profession practice in the field of severe and complex learning difficulties. Examples of recent research include developing children's social-cognitive awareness, multi-disciplinary assessment and personalised learning.

Parents

Working closely with parents is an aspiration of all schools and a continuing theme in government guidance. The *Special Educational Needs Code of Practice* (DfES, 2001a) devotes a chapter to 'Working in Partnership with Parents' and specific guidance on seeking to understand what parents might need is available (eg Greenwood, 2002).

Among the benefits of special schools to parents is that they can meet and gain support from other parents whose children have similar SEN. The school's work with parents is wide-ranging and can include:

- telephone contact, a daily home–school diary;
- whole school events such as special assemblies, concerts, exhibitions, visiting performers;
- newsletters;
- parent–teacher association;
- information evenings;
- workshops and training sessions, for example on behaviour management or approaches to reading or numeracy;
- annual review meetings;
- providing information about types of SEN and practical strategies for coping;
- putting parents in touch with support groups locally and nationally;
- making school premises available for various activities such as a parent support group;
- having displays of literature such as leaflets;
- being a 'one stop' point of contact for other services.

A model for collaborating with parents in order to help pupils experiencing difficulties at school is suggested by Hornby et al. (2003, p.131) and aspects merit consideration for a special school. It distinguishes between what it is considered parents 'need' and what it can reasonably be expected they can contribute. Parents' 'needs' are considered to be for communication with the school (which all parents need); liaison, such as that taking place at parent–teacher meetings (which most parents need); education, such as parents' workshops (which many need); and support, such as counselling (which some need). Parents' 'contributions' are considered as information, for example about the child's strengths (which all parents can provide); collaboration, for example with behaviour programmes or supporting a pupil's individual education plans (to which most parents could contribute); resources, such as being a classroom aid (to which many could contribute); and helping develop policy, for example, being a parent governor of the school (to which some could contribute). The model leaves open the exact interpretation of what the expressions 'most', 'many' and 'some' might mean.

The two examples below indicate the wide range of ways of involving parents (and also illustrates further ways of organising curriculum and assessment).

Emily Fortey School, Leicester

Emily Fortey School, Leicester is an LEA school educating 85 pupils aged 5 to 19 having SLD or PMLD. Primary and Senior classes are accommodated in the main school building where there is also a sensory stimulation room; a swimming pool (for hydrotherapy and conventional swimming lessons); and a technology room. The post-16 department in a separate block has two classrooms, a common room, and a kitchen area for teaching independence skills. Pupils are grouped according to age, within National Curriculum Key Stages, with no separate groups for specific disabilities and staffing allocated to classes according to their requirements.

The curriculum is structured into six core areas of communication (including early pre-verbal communication): mathematics, science, information technology, physical education, and personal and social education. The five enhancement areas are art, music, history, geography, and design technology. The core areas of the curriculum are each divided into three strands with each subject having: an early developmental learning curriculum for pupils with PMLD who may be working on sensory skills at a very early level; a skills curriculum of individual learning objectives as part of a pupil's IEP; and a knowledge curriculum offered as termly or half termly schemes of work to the whole class, giving pupils opportunities to practise and extend skills they are learning in the subject in the context of a range of activities within the schemes of work. The core areas are assessed through commercial tests, curriculum-related assessments and multi-professional assessments. The enhanced areas are taught as a rolling programme so that each subject is offered at least two terms out of three. A record is made of whether pupils have been working at an experiential, skills or concepts level in these subject areas.

Each pupil has a pupil records folder with recording sheets for each individual learning objective on their IEP, for each scheme of work and all assessments. Every pupil has an annual review of the targets in their IEP and an annual report of progress in all areas of the curriculum.

Parents can discuss their child's progress towards the targets in their IEP termly. Also, at the end of every week the school sends home a 'Record of Achievement' and 'Experience' sheet containing a sentence each on 'something I have been learning this week', 'something I have enjoyed this week' and 'something different I have been involved in this week'. A work sample, a photograph or a certificate to support these statements often accompanies this record. Evidence is collated in a Records of Achievement folder over the year, building up as the pupil progresses through the school.

Among other ways of involving parents are a daily home–school diary; telephone contact; an annual review meeting for each pupil at which progress over the last academic year is discussed and measurable targets are set for the next academic year; a class event held every term to which parents are invited; a termly whole-school event such as a special assembly, a concert, an exhibition or a visiting performer; a termly parents newsletter; a Parents Teachers Association; a termly Curriculum Information Evening for parents which are also an opportunity to meet with the child's class teacher to discuss progress; and an Asian mothers group which meet at a local community centre. From the age of 16 to 19, students follow a further education curriculum, which extends the work they have been doing in communication, mathematics, information and communications technology and physical education and also offers an accredited Learning for Life curriculum (AQA Unit Award Scheme). Students have opportunities to follow link courses at Colleges of Further Education.

The school aims to offer an inclusion link for all of its classes with a comparable aged class in a mainstream school. A term's project may lead up to a celebration of the work such as a performance, an exhibition, or an event for parents. Emily Fortey School has weekly whole-class inclusion links with several local schools and colleges.

Willoughby School, Lincolnshire

Willoughby School, Lincolnshire, purpose built in 1980 and undergoing a major extension of its buildings, is a co-educational special school educating 65 pupils aged 2 to 19 years having SLD or PMLD. Its provision ranges from the Bourne and District Portage Service, Portage, run by Willoughby staff, and early years intervention through to provision for post-19 students. The school is organised into four closely linked departments: the early

years/assessment department where pupils attend part time; a g
pupils with multi-sensory impairments; lower school for pupils aged 5 to 11
years; and upper school for pupils aged 11 to 19 years which has links with
the local college of further education. In teaching, pupils are encouraged to
discuss their work with adults and with each other; given opportunities to
choose their own equipment and materials to try to promote independent
learning; and encouraged to value the work of others.

Partnership with parents is strong and is encouraged through such developments as a home–school diary; telephone calls; parents working alongside
teachers in the classroom; newsletters; 'Open Door' sessions for parents
to discuss topics of particular interest or concern; information evenings;
consultation evenings; workshops on curriculum issues; a parent support
that meets monthly; and annual report to parents meeting.

Developing pupils' participation and communication

The *Special Educational Needs Code of Practice* (DfES, 2001a, especially
chapter 3) highlights the importance of pupil participation. A balance
is sought between encouraging participation and over-burdening the
pupil when he may not have sufficient experience and knowledge to make
judgements without support. Participation may include involvement in
developing individual education plans, setting educational targets, taking
part in school meetings such as schools council, as well as ensuring (through
such means as optimising communication) the pupils' fullest participation in
lessons and other activities.

To enhance pupils' communication, special schools provide a range of
approaches to help, depending upon the particular type of SEN. These include:

- speech and language therapy
- Picture Exchange Communication System (PECS)
- signing (Makaton, Signalong, British Sign Language for the Deaf)
- intensive interaction
- counselling
- arts therapies
- symbols, photographs, objects of reference
- augmentative communication
- social skills communicative training and role-play.

Linden Lodge School, Wandsworth is an example of a school working to ensure pupil communication is enhanced, as shown in the example below.

Linden Lodge School, Wandsworth

Linden Lodge School, Wandsworth (www.lindenlodge.wandsworth.sch.uk), whose history goes back to the opening in 1799 of the 'School for the Indigent Blind', is a co-educational day and weekly residential school with primary and secondary departments educating up to 95 pupils aged 3 to 19 years with VI/MDVI (visual impairment/multiple disabled visual impairment). It has residential accommodation, an indoor swimming pool and hydrotherapy pool, gymnasium and fitness suite, adventure playground, sensory garden, multi-sensory room and teaching areas. As a regional resource, the school supports pupils from over 34 LEAs. As well as a modified National Curriculum, the school provides a specialist curriculum including multi-sensory experiences, and a visual enhancement programme (eg specialised lighting, computer programmes and equipment) for pupils with residual vision. Mobility teachers teach pupils mobility and independence skills.

An extended Key Stage 4 for older pupils offers accredited courses including GCSE, Certificate of Educational Achievement and ASDAN. Residential provision includes a semi-independent house off-site where older pupils are encouraged to be as independent as possible. A school council comprises representatives from every secondary class and the oldest class of the primary department. The school employs a counsellor qualified and experienced in working with children and young people with visual impairments. It offers a range of opportunities supported by the Wandsworth Visual Impairment Service for some pupils to share experiences in a mainstream school or college. The service comprising specialist teachers and a mobility teacher is situated at the Lodge Family Centre, which is used as an assessment centre and for family support, at the entrance of the school.

Among the strengths of the school is its wide range of communication modes use, including objects of reference, the Picture Exchange Communication System (PECS), adapted Makaton body signing, and augmented speech devices. Modes for literacy include large print, Braille, Moon and picture symbols. A communications group including teachers and the speech and language therapist devise materials and strategies to develop this area of the specialist curriculum. A resource productions service transcribes print sources into alternative formats (including Braille, pre-Braille tactile materials, Moon, tactile diagrams, large print and picture symbols), maintains a standardised objects of reference library, and facilitates the use of information and communications technology. The ClearVision project of children's Braille and print books, custom-made tactile books and early Moon books, originally developed at Linden Lodge, and now a national charity, is sited in the school grounds.

Strategic links

Strategic planning and developments can involve formal links with other establishments and services to seek to offer a more comprehensive service. For example a school for pupils with behavioural, emotional and social difficulties can link with local pupil referral units and with psychiatric provision, as the example below outlines.

New Rush Hall, Ilford

New Rush Hall, Ilford (www.nrhs.redbridge.sch.uk) is a co-educational day school maintained by the London Borough of Redbridge for 60 pupils aged 5 to 16 years experiencing behavioural, emotional and social difficulties. The school was one of a small number of special schools chosen to be a 'Trailblazer' school in 2004.

Among the features contributing to pupils' behavioural, emotional and social progress is the emphasis on predictability where the school seeks to ensure that pupils recognise the consequences of their own behaviour, either positive or negative, on themselves and other people. At the end of each day there is a 'catch-up' session in which pupils who have not had a successful day have the opportunity to catch up on missed work, make reparations for behaviour such as writing a letter of apology, or evaluate their behaviour during the day. At the same time as this there is a 'team challenge' reward session for pupils who have had a more successful day. Accreditation opportunities include GCSEs and strong links are maintained with local schools (where some pupils who are progressing well behaviourally attend part time), and the local college of further education.

The school is part of the New Rush Hall Group, an educational organisation including, as well as the school, a behaviour support outreach team (offering consultation, observation, joint planning, feedback and advice to staff, individual and small group work, in-class support, team teaching, and training); three pupil referral units (one for pupils of all Key Stages, one for pupils in Key Stage 3, and one for pupils in Key Stage 4 the latter being based on two sites – a college of further education and a factory unit in Ilford); and an adolescent psychiatric unit. This aims to provide strategically for difficulties ranging from mild behaviour difficulties to mental health problems.

School self-evaluation and leadership and management

Where the pace of change is fast, it can be particularly difficult to establish secure structures for school self-evaluation. Effective and appropriate assessment and accreditation contribute to this, but other aspects of evaluation are also influential, for example, a responsive structure linking school and pupil requirements to staff training and support and staff performance management.

Approaches to using data on attainment and achievement in the broadest sense are outlined elsewhere and include their use for reviewing school provision such as staffing, resources, and the contribution of consultant professionals (Farrell, 2005a, pp.120–49); and target-setting in 'academic' subjects (pp.53–72) and in personal and social development (pp.73–89).

The *Every Child Matters'* 'five outcomes' for children and young people, readers may recall, are:

1 Staying healthy
2 Staying safe
3 Enjoying and achieving
4 Making a positive contribution, and
5 Achieving economic well-being.

These are integrated into the new OfSTED framework for the inspection of schools, where they are tracked into different elements of the school's provision (DfES/OfSTED, 2005, pp.18–20). For example, under, 'How well do learners achieve?', evaluation of 'the standards of learners' work in relation to their learning goals is taken as an indication of outcome 3, 'enjoying and achieving' (p.19). Similarly, under 'How well do programmes and activities meet the needs and interests of learners?', the evaluation of 'the extent to which the provision contributes to the learners' capacity to stay safe and healthy' relates to outcome 1 'staying healthy' and outcome 2 'staying safe' (p.20).

In the new framework for inspection (DfES/OfSTED, 2005), school self-evaluation plays a central part and is taken, among other things, to be an indication of effective leadership and management. It is hoped that the information and examples presented in this book will help special schools in their self-evaluation so that they will continue to develop and improve.

Thinking point

Readers may wish to consider:

• the extent to which the issues raised apply to a particular special school and how the school can best review its provision through school self-evaluation to ensure that it constantly strives for best practice.

Key texts

1   Department for Education and Skills/ Office for Standards in Education (2004) *A New Relationship with Schools: Improving Performance Through School Self-Evaluation* London, DfES/OfSTED.

This provides guidance on effective school improvement and its relationship to self-evaluation and on the OfSTED self-evaluation form.

2   Department for Education and Skills Office for Standards in Education (2005) *Every Child Matters: Framework for the Inspection of Schools in England from September 2005* London, OfSTED.

This covers the inspection system; the inspection process; the common inspection schedule for schools and other post-16 provision; and quality assurance (eg the code of conduct for inspectors).

10

Conclusion

I strongly believe that a Renaissance in special school education is possible that could to further excellence and progress for children. But to begin this resurgence, special schools and all involved with them must stand up for the best education for pupils – not political correctness.

Chapter 1 of this book considered inclusion and related statutory guidance; illustrated the types of special school in England; and indicated the quality of special schools and the numbers of pupils educated in them. Chapter 2: From Inclusion to Optimal Education, outlined some difficulties faced by that aspect of inclusion concerning reducing the number of pupils in special schools and increasing the number educated in mainstream schools. Weaknesses of inclusion were considered to relate to weakness of the social model of 'disability' and weaknesses of moral claims and empirical evidence. Instead of this, an approach of 'optimal education' was suggested. In Chapter 3, parents' views were illustrated while in Chapter 4 the views of pupils and ex-pupils of special schools were indicated.

Chapter 5 outlined examples of supportive LEAs. Chapters 6 and 7 showed the range and quality of pedagogy in special schools. Chapter 8 looked at outreach and in-reach while Chapter 9 concerned such issues as refining the curriculum, multi-professional working and other matters.

What might LEAs and special schools do to continue to improve?

The following questions are suggested for consideration by LEAs and special schools to assure their continued improvement.

LEAs checklist

1   Does the LEA have a clear statement expressing its support of good special schools, not only as agents to help and support pupils returning to mainstream school, but also as respected schools in their own right providing a valued and long-term education for pupils who benefit from this?

2   Does the LEA give parents a genuine choice of a range of special school provision, buying in to the special schools in other LEAs or in to non-maintained or independent special schools as necessary?

3   Does it monitor and evaluate the progress of pupils in special schools and compare this with the progress of pupils with similar SEN in mainstream school units and classrooms using measures of progress from baseline data?

4   Does the LEA invest money in special schools to ensure that their buildings, facilities and learning resources are of the highest quality?

5   Does the LEA involve special school staff in decision-making, policy development, providing and receiving training and other aspects of the LEAs work?

6   Does the LEA regard in-reach and outreach from special schools as having equal value?

7   Are there good links with non-maintained and independent special schools and maintained special schools in other areas that help ensure that the LEA is aware of best practice?

8   Is the LEA aware of the work of other LEAs that develop the work of special schools well?

Special schools checklist

1 Does the school have clear ways of identifying and assessing the pupils for whom it can best provide a suitable education?

2 Does the school have a range of approaches to teaching and learning that can be reasonably related to the particular special educational needs of the pupils it educates?

3 Do its assessment and accreditation systems challenge pupils yet ensure that they have opportunities to have their efforts recognised?

4 Assessment data used to help improve arrangements such as staffing, organisation and resources?

5 Assessment data used for whole cohort target-setting, bench-marking and value added measures so far as is practicable to help raise standards of achievement?

6 Are there well thought out and carefully evaluated ways of involving and supporting parents?

7 Is the school organisation and pupil grouping well-planned and is its effect monitored and evaluated?

8 Are the views and preferences of pupils regularly sought, listened to and acted upon as appropriate?

9 Are the views of parents regularly sought, listened to and acted upon as appropriate?

10 Is multi-professional working optimised through such approaches as joint assessments?

A final word

People educated in England are fortunate that there is a structure of National Curriculum and related assessments that enable standards of attainment and achievement to be known and therefore improved. Increasingly for pupils with SEN for whom the National Curriculum assessments may not give a full picture of their achievements, alternative assessments are being refined so that a better view is emerging about whether standards for pupils with SEN are high enough.

With this as a background, the work of special schools is being increasingly valued, their good work recognised and cherished by parents and pupils themselves. Long after the focus on inclusion has passed, the importance of education will remain and the contribution of special schools will help ensure that they maintain pride of place in the English education system.

Bibliography and References

Abberley, P. (1987) 'The concept of oppression and the development of social theory of disability' *Disability, Handicap and Society* 2:5–19.

Armstrong, D. (2003) *Experiences of Special Education: Re-evaluating Policy and Practice through Life Stories* London, Routledge-Falmer.

Bailey, J. (1998) 'Australia: Inclusion through categorisation' in T. Booth and M. Ainscow (eds) *From Them to Us: An International Study of Inclusion in Education* London, Routledge.

Barrow, Robin (2001) 'Inclusion vs. Fairness' *Journal of Moral Education* 30/3: 235–42.

Basic Skills Agency (2002) *Teaching Basic Skills in Special Schools* London, BSA.

Bellin, W. (1994) 'Caring Professions and Welsh-speakers: A Perspective from Language and Social Pathology' in Huws Williams, R., Williams, H. and Davies, E. (eds) *Gwaith Cymdeithasol a 'r Iaith Gymraeg/ Social Work in the Welsh Language* Cardiff, University of Wales Press.

Brewer, J. D. (1991) 'The Parallels Between Sectarianism and Racism: The Northern Ireland Experience' in CCETSW *One Small Step Towards Racial Justice* London, CCETSW.

Department for Education and Employment (1997) *Excellence for All Children: Meeting Special Educational Needs* London, DfEE.

Department for Education and Skills (2001a) *Special Educational Needs Code of Practice* London, DfES.

Department for Education and Skills (2001b) *Inclusive Schooling: Children with Special Educational Needs* London, DfES.

Department for Education and Skills (2003a) *Data Collection by Type of Special Educational Needs* London, DfES.

Department for Education and Skills (2003b) *The Report of the Special Schools Working Group* London, DfES.

Department for Education and Skills (2004a) *Removing Barriers to Achievement: The Government's Strategy for SEN* London, DfES.

Department for Education and Skills (2005) *National Statistic First Release: Special Educational Needs in England, January 2005 (SFR 24/2005)* DfES (www.dfes.gov.uk/rsgateway/DB/SFR/).

Department for Education and Skills/ Office for Standards in Education (2004) *A New Relationship with Schools: Improving Performance Through School Self-Evaluation* London, DfES/OfSTED.

Department for Education and Skills/ Office for Standards in Education (2005) *Every Child Matters: Framework for the Inspection of Schools in England from September 2005* London, DfES/OfSTED.

Farrell, M. (2003) *The Special School Handbook* London, David Fulton Publishers.

Farrell, M. (2004) *Special Educational Needs: A Resource for Practitioners* London, Paul Chapman Publishing.

Farrell, M. (2005a) *Key Issues in Special Education: Raising Standards of Pupils' Attainment and Achievement* London, Routledge.

Farrell, M. (2005b) *Inclusion at the Crossroads: Special Education – Concepts and Values* London, David Fulton Publishers.

Farrell, M. (2006a) *The Effective Teacher's Guide to Behavioural, Emotional and Social Difficulties* London, Routledge.

Farrell, M. (2006b) *The Effective Teacher's Guide to Moderate, Severe and Profound Learning Difficulties* London, Routledge.

Farrell, M. (2006c) *The Effective Teacher's Guide to Dyslexia and Other Specific Learning Difficulties* London, Routledge.

Farrell, M. (2006d) *The Effective Teacher's Guide to Autism and Other Communication Difficulties* London, Routledge.

Farrell, M. (2006e) *The Effective Teacher's Guide to Sensory Impairment and Physical Disability* London, Routledge.

Gallagher, D. J. (2001) 'Neutrality as a moral standpoint, conceptual confusion and the full inclusion debate' *Disability and Society* 16/5: 637–54.

Greenwood, C. (2002) *Understanding the Needs of Parents: Guidelines for Effective Collaboration with Parents of Children with Special Educational Needs* London, David Fulton Publishers.

Habermas, J. (1987) *The Theory of Communicative Action: Volume 2 Lifeworld and System* Boston, Beacon Press.

Hegarty, S. (2001) 'Inclusive education – a case to answer' *Journal of Moral Education* 30/3: 243–9.

Hornby, G., Hall, E. and Hall, C. (2003) *Counselling Pupils in Schools: Skills and Strategies for Teachers* London, Routledge.

Jones, C. (1998) 'Social Work and Society' in Adams, R., Dominelli, L. and Payne, M. (eds) *Social Work: Themes, Issues and Critical Debates* London, Macmillan Press.

Lindsay, G. (2003) 'Inclusive education: a critical perspective' *British Journal of Special Education* 3/1:3–12.

Locke, John (1690) *Two Treatise on Government* (many editions).

MacKay, G. (2002) 'The disappearance of disability? Thoughts on a changing culture' *British Journal of Special Education* 29/4, December 2002.

Manset, G. and Semmel, M. I. (1997) 'Are inclusive programmes for students with mild disabilities effective? A comparative review of model programmes' *Journal of Special Education* 31/2:155–80.

Marston, D. (1996) 'A comparison of inclusion only, pull-out only and combined service models for students with mild disabilities' *Journal of Special Education* 30/2:121–32.

Mills, P. E., Cole, K. N., Jenkins, J. R. and Dale, P. S. (1998) 'Effects of differing levels of inclusion on pre-schoolers with disabilities' *Exceptional Children* 65: 79–90.

National Association for Non-Maintained and Independent Special Schools (NASS) (2005a) *Pace and Progression Pilot – Achievement and Attainment Tables 2004* London, NASS.

National Association for Non-Maintained and Independent Special Schools (NASS) (2005b) *Secondary School Achievement Tables 2004* London, NASS.

Newport, F. (2004) *Outreach Support from Special Schools* Taunton, South West SEN Regional Partnership.

OfSTED/Equal Opportunities Commission (1996) *The Gender Divide* London, Her Majesty's Stationary Office.

Office for Standards in Education (2000) *Evaluating Educational Inclusion: Guidance for Inspectors and Schools* London, OfSTED.

Oliver, M. (1996) *Understanding Disability: From Theory to Practice* London, Macmillan/Palgrave.

Powers, S., Gregory, S. and Thoutenhoofd, D. (1999) 'The educational achievement of deaf children' *Deafness and Education International* 1/1:1–9.

Qualifications and Curriculum Authority (2001a) *Planning, teaching and assessing the curriculum for pupils with learning difficulties: Mathematics* London, QCA.

Qualifications and Curriculum Authority (2001b) *Supporting the Target-setting Process* London, QCA.

Richardson, D. and Robinson, V. (1997) *Introducing Women's Studies* London, Macmillan Press (second edition).

Rouse, M. and Florian, L. (1997) 'Inclusive education in the market place' *International Journal of Inclusive Education* 1: 323–36.

Sapsted, D. (2004) 'TV is human right says tree row man' *The Daily Telegraph* 31 May 2004 p.6 cols 6–7.

Sebba, J. and Sachdev, D. (1997) *What Works in Inclusive Education?* Ilford, Barnardos.

Sheehy, K., Rix, J., Nind, M. and Simmons, K. (2004) 'Perspectives on inclusive education: learning from each other' *Support for Learning* 19/3: 137–41.

Skellington, R. (1996) *'Race' in Britain Today* London, Sage (second edition).

Thompson, N. (1992) *Existentialism and Social Work* Aldershot, Avebury.

Thompson, N. (1995) *Age and Dignity: Working with Older People* Aldershot, Arena.

Thompson, N. (1998) *Promoting Equality: Challenging Discrimination and Oppression in the Human Services* London, Macmillan Press.

Thompson, N. (2001) *Anti-Discriminatory Practice* Basingstoke, Palgrave (third edition).

Tilstone, C. Florian, L. and Rose, R. (eds) (1998) *Promoting Inclusive Practice* London, Routledge.

Vaughan, S. and Klinger, J. K. (1998) 'Students' perceptions of inclusion and resource room settings' *Journal of Special Education* 32/2: 79–88.

Warnock, M. (2005) 'Special educational needs: a new look' *Impact No. 11* London, The Philosophy of Education Society of Great Britain.

Wilmot, D. (2006) 'Educational Inclusion and Special Schooling within a Local Education Authority' Thesis submitted for the degree of Doctor in Education (EdD) University of Birmingham.

Wise, S. (2000) 'Heterosexism' in Davies, M. (ed.) (2000) *The Blackwell Encyclopaedia of Social Work* Oxford, Blackwell.

World Health Organisation (2001) ICF-International Classification of Functioning, Disability and Health Geneva, WHO.

Appendices

Addresses

National Association of Independent Schools and Non-Maintained Special
Schools (NASS)
PO Box 705
York Y030 6WW
Tel: 01845 522542
email: georginacarney@btinternet.com
www.nasschools.org.uk

The NASS is a membership association working with and for special schools
in the voluntary sector within the United Kingdom. It provides information,
support and training to it members through a range of media to benefit and
advance the education of young people with SEN.

Rescare
Rayner House
23 Higher Hillgate
Stockport
Cheshire
SK1 3ER
Tel: 0161 474 7323
Fax : 0161 480 3668
email: office@rescare.org.uk
www.rescare.org.uk

A national society for children and adults with learning disabilities and their
families, Rescare promotes choice in education through properly resourced
mainstream, special day and residential schools. The charity campaigns
for the retention and development of special schools. Run by families
for families, it represents thousands of families and has affiliations in
New Zealand and Australia. Its national office in England provides
advice and support through publications and personal contacts. Rescare
organises public meetings and workshops and offers a help-line and a
welfare service.

Internet sites

The following are a sample of Internet sites involved in supporting special schools.

www.gsspl.org.uk

Gloucestershire Special School Protection League has launched a national campaign to, 'prevent the culling of special schools in the name of inclusion'. Has links leading to other sites supporting special schools.

www.vips-in-sen.co.uk

Voice of Independent Parents in Special Educational Needs. Parents action group based in Richmond Upon Thames one of whose aims is to, 'protect the decreasing number of excellent special school provision'.

www.kingsdownparents.co.uk

Parents fighting to save the Kingsdown School, Eastwood, Essex.

www.saveourschools.co.uk

Parents fighting against special school closures in Leicester.

www.senaction.com

Against the London Borough of Bromley and the LEA over inclusion for children with SEN until the child can cope and there is parental agreement.

www.spiritofwinchelsea.co.uk

Parents of pupils at Winchelsea School, Poole, Dorset, fighting closure by the LEA.

www.dsspl.co.uk

Dudley special school protection league.

Abbreviations

ADHD	attention deficit hyperactivity disorder
ALL	Accreditation for Life and Living
ASD	autistic spectrum disorder
ASDAN	Award Scheme Development and Accreditation Network
BESD	behavioural, emotional and social difficulties
DfEE	Department of Education and Employment
DfES	Department for Education and Skills
FLAME	Function, Language And Movement Education
GCSE	General Certificate of Secondary Education
GNVQ	General National Vocational Qualifications
HI	hearing impairment
IEP	Individual Education Plan
LEA	local education authority
MLD	moderate learning difficulty
MOVE	Movement Opportunities Via Education
NASS	National Association for Non-Maintained and Independent Special Schools
NVQ	National Vocational Qualifications
OfSTED	Office for Standards in Education
PECS	Picture Exchange Communication System
PIVATs	Performance Indicators for Value Added Target Setting
PLASC	Pupil Level Annual School Census
PMLD	profound and multiple learning difficulty
PSHCE	personal, social, health and citizenship education
QCA	Qualification and Curriculum Authority
RNIB	Royal National Institute for the Blind
SEN	special educational needs
SENCO	special educational needs co-ordinator
SLD	severe learning difficulty
TEACCH	Teaching and Education of Autistic Children and Communication Handicap
VI	visual impairment

Index